*The Spiritual Direction of
Saint Claude de la Colombière*

The Spiritual Direction of Saint Claude de la Colombière

Translated and arranged by
Mother M. Philip, I.B.V.M.
The Bar Convent, York

IGNATIUS PRESS   SAN FRANCISCO

Original English edition: *The Spiritual Direction of
Blessed Claude de la Colombière*
Translated and arranged by Mother M. Philip, I.B.V.M.
The Bar Convent, York, England
© 1934, Burns Oates & Washbourne, Ltd., London
With ecclesiastical approval

Cover by Roxanne Mei Lum

Printed in 1998 Ignatius Press, San Francisco
ISBN 0-89870-682-3
Library of Congress catalogue number 97-76860
Printed in the United States of America ∞

CONTENTS

PART II

DIRECTION SUITABLE FOR RELIGIOUS

FOREWORD TO
THE SECOND EDITION

THE Encyclical Letter of Pope Pius XII, "On Devotion to the Sacred Heart of Jesus", 1956, opens with the glorious and joyous words of Isaiah the Prophet, "You shall draw waters with joy out of the Savior's fountains." The Church applies this passage to the Sacred Heart of Jesus and the abundance of heavenly gifts poured out on mankind.

Certainly, one of the great gifts given to the Church is the Jesuit saint Claude La Colombière. This saint shared the same century with St. Margaret Mary Alacoque, the Visitation sister who received the visions of the Sacred Heart which Catholic scholars hail as the modern period of the devotion. This holy Jesuit—with a reputation already for brilliance in teaching, preaching, and spiritual direction—was sent by Christ to encourage spiritually and support the humble nun struggling with the great revelations of God's love and mercy found in the pierced heart of the Savior. His wise spiritual counsel steadied St. Margaret Mary and gave her the confidence and discernment to reveal and promote the revelation of the Sacred Heart as our Lord wished.

St. Claude collaborated with the revelation by preaching missions, giving retreats on the Sacred Heart, and by making his own consecration to the Sacred Heart. Claude carried this revelation all the way to England, ministering to persecuted Catholics, but had to return to France, his health broken.

In our century, we are privileged to see more evidence of the Sacred Heart's abundant gifts. Claude's canonization as a saint was made possible as the result of a miraculous cure of a Jesuit, a former missionary, who like Claude had been persecuted and exiled for the Faith.

With the re-publication of St. Claude's spiritual directions to various men and women, we find the contemporary Church being blessed with the same wisdom that contributed to the formation of two saints and countless others, down to ourselves. In this century, typified by a struggle so cataclismic that it is characterized as the war between a Civilization of Love and the Culture of Death, we look forward to the spiritual vision of Claude imbued with confidence and trust in God's mercy and love.

The Vatican II document, *Lumen Gentium,* echoing the Gospel, calls the People of God to universal holiness. Of those waters that we in the contemporary

Church draw from the side of Christ is St. Claude's spiritual wisdom in this little book, assisting us in the call to holiness. May it find a wide and attentive audience.

John Galten
Director, Saint Ignatius Institute
San Francisco

INTRODUCTION

*Adapted from an introduction to
"Blessed Claude de la Colombière and souls",
by the Rev. Fr. Monier-Vinard, S.J.*

As a preacher, moralist, or writer Blessed Claude de la
Colombière* may be equalled or surpassed; but as a
director of souls he ranks among the masters of the
spiritual life.

Our Lord said to Saint Margaret Mary: "Father de la
Colombière's talent is to lead souls to God." This talent
which shines so clearly in the work and life of the Saint
is not merely a gift, but the result of nature and grace.
A clever psychologist, he easily read the hearts of others;
he excelled in analyzing his own interior life and saw
clearly into that of others. His sure judgment enabled
him to understand the difficulties of each soul, and he
knew how to make each accept and carry out his advice,
which was always to the point.

Above all he was a saint.

A long and virile experience of virtue had given him

*Claude de la Colombière was canonized by Pope John Paul II
on May 31, 1992 – ED.

the personal experience necessary to be a director. His letters show that his advice was brief, decisive, and deep. He tried to inspire souls with an energetic and stable will to serve God, cost what it might, and never to refuse anything to the Divine Majesty. Then he guided this will lovingly toward God's will, helping it to accept all that Providence permitted with resignation and joy.

Many directors have spoken the same language to their penitents, but few have been listened to so attentively and followed so faithfully.

This, Blessed Claude records himself in a letter to Mother de Saumaise written after his return to France from London in 1679. He writes of a visit he had just paid to Paray-le-Monial:

> I cannot tell you what great consolation I had. I found things going on admirably; it seems to me that everything has improved since my departure. I do not know how many people there are whom I had quite forgotten, in whom God has allowed seed to fructify beyond all my hopes, so that they now practice solid virtue with admirable constancy. As you may imagine I had not time in one week for long interviews with all who wished to speak to me, yet it pleased God's infinite mercy so to bless the few words I said, that everyone was satisfied and renewed in fervor. . . .

There was nothing "booky" about Blessed Claude's direction; it came from his heart and reached the soul still burning with his love for God. You felt that he lived what he counselled, and that following his Master, he asked nothing of souls that he would not be the first to do himself.

N.B.—The full text of Claude de la Colombière's Journal of Retreats, Lyons, 1674, and London, 1677, is to be found in his life, *A Jesuit at the English Court,* published by Burns Oates & Washbourne.

PART ONE

ON HOLY MASS

Spiritual Reflections

GOD is more honored by a single Mass than he could be by all actions of angels and men together, however fervent and heroic they might be. Yet how few hear Mass with the intention of giving God this sublime honor! How few think with joy on the glory a Mass gives to God. How few rejoice to possess the means of honoring him as he deserves! How seldom do we thank Jesus Christ that, in doing away with all other sacrifices, he has left us a sacrifice that cannot fail to be pleasing to God, a thank-offering proportionate to the benefits we have received from him, a victim capable of effacing the sins of the world.

It may be that in praying, fasting, and giving alms I offend God by my bad intention or by the way I act, more than I glorify him. Perhaps my acts of penance merit punishment rather than cancel it, and my alms render me a still greater debtor to God; but when I hear Mass, when I offer the Holy Sacrifice as priest or as a member of the Church, I can with full courage and confidence defy heaven to do anything that pleases God more. Then I can ask for pardon and be sure of obtaining it no matter how great or numberless my sins. Whatever I hope for and desire I can pray for confidently. I can ask for great graces of every kind for myself, my friends, and my enemies, and far from being ashamed at asking for so much I shall know it is little in comparison with what I offer. My only fear is that I shall ask too little and not have a firm, unshakeable hope of obtaining not only what I ask but far more.

If we only knew the treasure we hold in our hands! Happy a thousand times those who know how to profit by the Mass! In this adorable Sacrifice they can find all things: graces, riches spiritual and temporal, favors for body and mind for life and eternity.

Yet how often we must confess that we do not even think of using the treasure we possess, we do not even try to grasp it. What value do we set upon holy Mass? With what intentions do we assist at it? How do we hear it? Some come from custom and human respect, and sometimes even from less worthy motives. At Mass they are occupied with useless thoughts; they amuse themselves with looking at the decorations of the church or at the people; they talk and even yawn, not knowing how to occupy themselves.

Have you never received any favors from God, and have you thanked him for them? Take care lest through lack of gratitude you prevent God from showering his blessings upon you. It is a strange thing that we who are surrounded and loaded with God's blessings, we whom God has loved, preserved, and cherished from the first moment of our life until now, have never even thanked him as we ought.

This we can do in holy Mass!

ON HOLY COMMUNION

Letter 146. London, 1678

IT matters very little if you approach the Sacraments with sensible fervor, provided that you replace this with deep and sincere humility. Without this humility there is nothing more despicable in God's eyes than ourselves, but with it we can go to him without fear, certain that he will deign to look on us with infinite mercy.

Letter 136. London, 1678

Despise temptations against faith and remember that you believe what so many saints and doctors have believed.

Your usual intention at Communion should be that of Jesus Christ in coming to you, for it is the purest and most excellent possible: to unite yourself to the source and object of love, to strengthen yourself in the service of God and in the practice of virtue, to purify yourself by union with him who is Purity itself. You can add special intentions to these according to your needs and obligations.

Spiritual Notes. Lyons, 1674

Why was the purity of Mary so great but because she was to bear the Son of God in her womb. If she had not been purer than the angels, it would not have been seemly for the Word to dwell in her; he would not have taken such delight in her, nor would he have brought her the precious gifts with which he filled her at the moment of the Incarnation. In Holy Communion we receive the same Jesus Christ that Mary bore for nine months in her womb. What is our purity? What care do we take to prepare our soul? We sometimes commit faults on the eve, on the day, and even in the very act of receiving Communion. Yet Jesus comes to us! How kind he is! "Depart from me, O Lord, for I am a sinful man" (Lk 5:8). Can God delight to come to me? Is he not repulsed at the sight of my misery? Yet I go to him without shame, confusion, or contrition.

O my God, I will try so to prepare my heart that you may take pleasure and delight in it, and so that I may not place any obstacle to the immense graces I shall receive if I purify myself and realize what great good I shall lose if I do not do so.

Retreat Notes. Lyons, 1674

I was greatly touched in considering the thoughts that Jesus Christ has of me when I hold him in my hands:

the dispositions of his Heart, his desires and plans for my soul. What sweetness and grace a pure and detached soul receives in this Sacrament.

Letter 73. London, 1678

You still doubt as to whether you ought to go to Holy Communion. Do you not see that these troubles which precede your Communions come from the evil spirit who abhors them and that the moments of peace which follow them come from the Spirit of God who loves them. I am surprised that you can hesitate about it; it is as clear as daylight; without this help you would be lost. Far from dissuading you from going to Communion, I would advise you to increase the number of times you go.

Spiritual Reflections

All spiritual writers agree that the best sign you can have of solid devotion is the amendment of life and perseverance in good. You think there is illusion in such frequent Communion and that it would be better to go more rarely. Do not come to me with such arguments. I began to amend my life by frequenting Holy Communion after having tried every other way and failed. When I went rarely to Holy Communion I had no end of bad habits and imperfections which appeared to me insurmountable. I uprooted these by multiplying my Communions, and you want me to believe that it was the devil who urged me to do this! Every time I omitted to frequent Communion I felt my weakness more. I know some souls who have relapsed into sin the very day they omitted Communion. When I communicated again I felt fervor rekindle in my heart. I know by my own experience and by that of hundreds of people that by following your advice they would soon give up all reception of the Sacraments.

No fervent soul has ever relaxed who did not first leave off receiving the Holy Eucharist. If I found that when going frequently to Communion I became no better, was still just as weak, just as prone to evil, just as indifferent about sin, I should conclude, not that I ought to leave off going, but that I ought to receive Our Lord with better dispositions. I should see if my confessions were wanting in sincerity, contrition, or purpose of amendment.

If you are sinful, repent so that you can communicate often. If you are imperfect, go often to Communion that you may amend your faults.

Retreat Notes. Lyons, 1674

My daily Mass and Communion is my only hope and resource. Jesus Christ can do very little if he cannot uphold me from day to day. He will not fail to reproach me if I begin to relax; each day he will counsel me and give me new strength; he will instruct, console, and encourage me and give me all the graces for which I pray.

ON CONFESSION AND SPIRITUAL DIRECTION

Spiritual Reflections

I AM not so astonished at those souls who fear confession because they do not want to give up their sins, as I am of those who fear it because they are frightened of making known their sins. The proof that the latter is a temptation is that it is to be found in people quite unknown to the confessor and in those whom he will never know. What does the priest know after the confession except that there is a person who has committed sin. You do yourself no more harm than if you confessed to a statue. The more the confessor knows you, the more he will esteem you; the more difficulty you have, the more he must value the confidence you have in him and be touched that you have told him the one thing in the world you would naturally wish to hide. The worse the sin is, and the better the confessor knows you, the more merit you gain, therefore if he is reasonable the more he must esteem you, at any rate if he has feelings at all like those of God and the angels who see your humility with joy and admiration. What madness it would be for a confessor to condemn you in his heart when God absolves you and fills you with his grace. If he is unchristian and a fool, he will have these sentiments, but if he is reasonable and has faith, he will admire you and praise God while humbling himself.

Letter 27. London, 1677

You should make up your mind once for all to choose one person to whom you make known your interior life. To change one's director every year is equivalent to never making any progress.

Half an hour a month in which to give an account of your prayer and dispositions should suffice and would be real direction: for it is mere waste of time and real illusion to expect endless visits which recommence daily; self is satisfied, and self is distracted by so much talk, but God is left alone and it is with him alone that we ought to try and be united.

We must take care not to be so occupied with ourself that we try to interest everyone in our soul, while at the same time we do not think of God who alone ought to occupy our love, so that we go to him with simplicity, without so much thought of self and without bothering others by so much talk about ourself.

ON PRAYER

Retreat Notes. Lyons, 1674

As I feel a great attraction toward prayer I asked God, by Our Lady's intercession, to give me the grace to go on increasing in love of this holy exercise until my death. It is the only means of purifying us, of uniting us to God, and of allowing God to unite himself to us and be glorified in us. We must pray to obtain the apostolic virtues; pray that we may use them to help others, and pray also that we may not lose them while serving others. The counsel: pray without ceasing, seems sweet to me and in no way impossible. It includes the practice of the presence of God, and with his help I resolve to follow it. We always have need of God, therefore we must always pray. The more we pray, the more we please him and the more we obtain. I do not ask for consolation in prayer; that God gives where he chooses; I am not worthy of consolation and am too weak to bear it. Extraordinary graces are not good for me; to give them to me would be like building upon sand, or pouring a precious liquid into a broken vase. I ask God to give me a solid, simple gift of prayer which will glorify him and not make me vain. It seems to me that dryness and desolation accompanied by grace are very useful to me, for then I delight in making acts of real virtue: I strive against my bad inclinations and try to be faithful to God.

Retreat Notes. Lyons, 1674

When we are distracted during prayer and find the time long because of our impatience to pass on to something else, it is good to say to yourself: My soul, art thou tired of thy God? Art thou not satisfied with him? Thou possessest him and dost thou seek for something else? Where canst thou be better than in his company? Where canst thou profit more? I have experienced that this calms the mind and unites it with God.

Retreat Notes. Lyons, 1674

How can we help our neighbor? By prayer and good works. Preaching is useless without grace, and grace is only obtained by prayer. If conversions are few, it is because few pray. Prayer for souls is so pleasing to God, it is as though we asked a mother to forgive her son.

Letter 143. Lyons, 1679

In prayer always follow the attraction of your heart, whether God draws you to consider Our Lord's Passion or the joys of heaven; you cannot do wrong in that.

Letter 138. London, 1678

The best book of meditation on the Passion is the Passion itself in the Gospel: read this and meditate upon it, reflecting upon the love and patience of Jesus Christ.

Letter 135. London, 1677

Continue to pray as you feel drawn, but do not worry about it, for worry comes from self-love. You must abandon yourself to the leading of God with no other intention than that of pleasing him, and when you know that you have this intention deep in your heart, you must not waste time in reflecting about yourself and about the degree of virtue you have attained; occupy yourself with him whom you love and bother very little about yourself.

Letter 132. London, 1677

In general, the mere sense of the presence of God is an excellent prayer, and if you can occupy yourself with it without strain, you need think of nothing else: not that you must avoid making acts when drawn to do so, but do not worry about them unless for some reason you feel constrained to make them. Go to God simply, with great confidence that his goodness will guide you; let yourself go confidently as your heart draws you, and fear nothing but pride and self-love.

Letter 126. London, 1678

As for prayer, confine yourself to admiring the perfections of God and the virtues of the saints and bear your involuntary distractions patiently. I assure you, you will gain great merit. Enjoy, cherish, and increase the desire God gives you of doing something for him. Make this the subject of your prayer as often as you feel moved to do so. Do not seek another subject unless you have no good thought at all in your heart. If you are moved by sentiments of admiration, desire, shame, sorrow, submission, contempt of the world, and love of God, you can do without books.

Letter 120. London, 1679

About prayer:—I think you cling too closely to the points given in the book: nevertheless if to do so helps you, do not change. Remember that every time you are filled with feelings out of the ordinary, whether of thanksgiving, love, admiration of God's goodness, desire of pleasing him, contempt for things of this world, or the thought of his presence, you must make these things the subject of your prayer and try to relish and increase these sentiments.

Letter 98. Lyons, 1680

During prayer and at other times keep yourself as far as possible at the feet of Jesus Christ, as the most imperfect and wretched of all his creatures and as one who deserves hell. But do not fail to put all your confidence in him, and never fear that he will reject you on account of your infidelities. You know quite well that he seeks those who offend him and that it was for sinners that he became Man. Do not leave his adorable feet; cling so closely to them, that if he wanted to condemn you to hell, he would, as it were, be obliged to go with you.

When you can do nothing at prayer, make acts of humility, comparing your nothingness with God's greatness, your ingratitude with his benefits, your lack of virtue with the purity and perfection of the saints.

Letter 74. London, 1677

It is a great illusion, but a very common one, to imagine that one has little or great virtue according to the many or few distractions one has in prayer! I have known souls raised to a high degree of contemplation who were distracted from the beginning to the end of their prayer. Most of the people who are so much troubled at this wandering of the mind are souls filled with self-love who cannot bear the confusion into which it throws them before God and man and who cannot put up with the weariness and fatigue their prayer causes them. They desire to be rewarded by sensible consolation for the mortification they practice.

Letter 22. London, 1676

Do not be either astonished or discouraged at the difficulties you find in prayer. Only be constant and submissive and God will be pleased with you. Perhaps the lights you have concerning your unworthiness are graces by which God prepares you for the dryness that follows, which is a punishment for past infidelities.

Letter 122. London, 1678

Neither prayer nor recollection call for strain: faults must be avoided, and we must be united to God in heart if we cannot be in mind. Love and do what you will. Nothing is difficult to him who loves, and he only has to make efforts to feel his love. I say feel because it is not even necessary always to express it in prayer. He whom you love sees your heart and that is sufficient. He does not want you to worry about your lack of power to act and to produce affections as easily as you would like. You must submit humbly to his will in this, judging yourself unworthy to raise your thoughts to him. Oh, how happy you would be if you would learn this lesson well and so place your soul in holy liberty and in perfect resignation to God's guidance of you.

Letter 142. Lyons, 1679

The coldness you feel in prayer comes from your too
great desire for sensible fervor. You must love God
alone with all your heart and be ready to be satisfied
with his Cross as the only sign of his love. Take the
posture which inconveniences you the least and take
care to pray quietly and not to strain yourself.

Letter 141. London, 1678

When you have no consolation in prayer you must
endure your impatience to finish it with great humility
and stay rather longer than usual so as to mortify
yourself.

Letter 138. London, 1678

Despise troublesome thoughts and bear their importunity with resignation. A soul that fears God is not
troubled by her fear of committing faults; she goes to
her good Master with great liberty of spirit and childlike confidence. When we only desire to please him, we
must not fear that he is offended by things that we
believe to be well done. Keep yourself as much as
possible in the presence of God, humbly tasting the
sweetness you will find there: do not fear illusion.

Take great care not to omit your prayer unless you
are ill; if you cannot kneel, sit down: it is all the same.

ON DEVOTION TO THE SACRED HEART

Retreat Notes. London, 1677

I HAVE understood that God wants me to serve him by procuring the accomplishment of his desires concerning the devotion that he revealed to a person* to whom he communicates himself very intimately and for which he has willed to use my weakness. I have already suggested this devotion to many people in England, and I have written to France asking one of my friends to propagate it in the place in which he lives; it will be very fruitful there; the large number of faithful souls in the community makes me believe that its practice in that house will be very pleasing to God.

O my God, why cannot I be everywhere so as to let all know what thou expectest from thy servants and friends!

God having revealed himself to the person whom we may believe to be according to his Heart on account of the great graces he gives her, she told me about it, and I obliged her to write down what she had told

*Saint Margaret Mary Alacoque.

me; this I have copied into my Retreat Journal because God wishes to use my weakness for the fulfillment of his plans.

Being before the Blessed Sacrament one day of its octave, I received from my God signal tokens of his love, and I felt urged with the desire of making him some return, and of rendering him love for love. "Thou canst not make me a greater return of love", he said, "than by doing what I have so often asked of thee." Then, discovering to me his divine Heart, he said: "Behold this Heart which has loved men so much, that it has spared nothing, even to exhausting and consuming itself, in order to testify to them its love; and in return I receive from the greater number nothing but ingratitude by reason of their irreverence and sacrileges, and by the coldness and contempt which they show me in this Sacrament of Love. But what I feel most keenly is that it is hearts which are consecrated to me that treat me thus. Therefore I ask of thee that the Friday after the octave of Corpus Christi be set apart for a special feast to honor my Heart, by communicating on that day and making reparation to it by a solemn act, so as to make amends for the indignities which it has received during the time it has been exposed on the altars. I promise thee that my Heart shall expand itself to shed in abundance the influence of its divine love upon those who shall thus honor it and cause it to be honored."

"But, my Lord, to whom art thou speaking? To a creature so despicable, to so miserable a sinner, that her unworthiness will hinder the accomplishment of thy designs?"

"What", replied Our Lord, "dost thou not know that

I make use of the weak to confound the strong; and that it is generally in the least and the poorest of spirit that I make my power shine forth most strikingly, that they may attribute nothing to themselves?"

"Give me then," I said to him, "give me the means of doing what thou commandest."

Then he said to me: "Go to my servant, N,* and tell him from me to exert himself to the utmost to establish this devotion and to give this pleasure to my Heart. Let him not be discouraged at the difficulties he will encounter, for they will be many; but let him know that he is all-powerful who places no confidence in himself, but trusts entirely to me."

Letter 5. 1679

I recommend you to go to Holy Communion the day after the octave of Corpus Christi in reparation for all the irreverence shown to Jesus Christ while he has been exposed on all the altars of the Catholic world during this octave. This practice was recommended to me by a person of extraordinary sanctity who assured me that all those who give Our Lord this sign of love will derive great fruit from it. Try gently to induce your friends to do the same thing. I hope many communities will begin this devotion this year and always continue it.

*This, of course, was Father de la Colombière himself.

Retreat Notes. Lyons, 1674

The love of Our Lord's Heart was in no way diminished by the treason of Judas, the flight of the apostles, and the persecution of his enemies. Jesus was only grieved at the harm they did themselves; his sufferings helped to assuage his grief because he saw in them a remedy for the sins committed by his enemies. The Sacred Heart was full of most tender love: there was no bitterness in it; no cruelty and injustice that he received moved it to feelings other than those of compassion and affection.

I turned to Mary and asked her to obtain for me the grace to imitate Our Lord's Heart. I saw how perfectly her heart copied his: she loved those who put her Son to death and offered him to God the Father for them. This enkindled a very great love of virtue in my heart.

O sacred Hearts of Jesus and of Mary, truly worthy of possessing all hearts and of reigning over men and angels, you shall be my models; I will try to copy you. May my heart live always in the Hearts of Jesus and Mary, and may their hearts live in mine, so that I may never do anything that is not in accordance with them.

Retreat Notes. London, 1677

This offering is made in honor of the divine Heart, the seat of all virtues, the source of all blessing, the refuge of all holy souls.

The principal virtues to be honored in him are:

First, his ardent love for the Eternal Father joined to a profound reverence and to the greatest possible humility.

Secondly, an infinite patience, an extreme sorrow and contrition for all the sins which he took upon himself; the confidence of a tender son joined to the shame of a great sinner.

Thirdly, a very real compassion for our miseries, an immense love for us in spite of all we are, an unalterable tranquillity of soul based on such perfect conformity to God's will that nothing disturbed it however opposed it appeared to be to his zeal and humility, and even to his love.

This Heart is still the same, always burning with love for men, always open so as to shower down graces and blessings upon us, always touched by our sorrows, always eager to impart its treasures to us and to give himself to us, always ready to receive us, to be our refuge, our dwelling place, and our heaven even in this world.

In return it finds in so many hearts nothing but hardness, forgetfulness, contempt, and ingratitude: Jesus loves and is not loved; his love is not even known because we will not deign to receive the gifts by which he proves his love or listen to the secret and tender words of love that he wishes to speak to our hearts.

(Père Croiset, S.J., says that the following Act of Consecration is, except for a few slight changes, the one used by Saint Claude when he consecrated himself to the Sacred Heart at Paray-le-Monial on June 21, 1675.)

In reparation for so many outrages and for such cruel ingratitude, O adorable and loving Heart of my very loving Jesus, and that I may do all in my power to prevent myself from falling into such misery, I offer thee my heart; I give myself entirely to thee, and from this hour I sincerely desire to forget myself and all that concerns me so that I may do away with this barrier that prevents me from entering into this Divine Heart that thou hast so lovingly opened to me, and in which I long to enter so that I may live and die with thy most faithful servants, penetrated through and through and even consumed by thy love.

To thy Heart I offer all the merit and satisfaction of every Mass and prayer, of all the mortifications and religious exercises, of all acts of zeal, humility, and obedience and of all other virtues that I shall practice till the last moment of my life. Not only do I offer this to honor thy most loving Heart, but I very humbly beg of thee to accept the entire offering I make thee, to use it as thou wilt and in favor of whom thou wilt. As I have already given all the satisfactory merit of my actions to the souls in purgatory, I desire now that it be given to them according to the will of thy Heart, O Jesus.

This will not prevent me from fulfilling my obligations of saying Mass and of praying for certain intentions that obedience prescribes; nor will it prevent me from saying Masses for poor people, nor for my relations and friends who may ask me to do so; but as I shall then be using something which does not belong to me, I wish, as is but just, the obedience, charity, and other virtues that I shall practice on these occasions to belong entirely to thy Sacred Heart from whence I shall have drawn the grace necessary to perform these virtues which therefore necessarily belong entirely to thee.

Retreat Notes. London, 1677

Most Sacred Heart of Jesus, do thou teach me an entire forgetfulness of myself, since there is no other way of entering into thee. As all that I do in future will belong entirely to thee, grant that I may do nothing which is not worthy of thee. Teach me what I must do to attain to pure love of thee, with the desire of which thou hast inspired me. I feel in myself a great wish to please thee and a still greater inability to do so without a special light and help which I can look for only from thee. Do thy will in me, O Lord; I oppose it I know, but I would fain not do so. It is for thee to do all, O divine Heart of

Jesus; thou alone wilt have all the glory of my sanctification if I become a saint. This is self-evident to me, but it will be a great glory for thee, and it is for this alone that I desire to be perfect. Amen.

ACT OF CONSECRATION TO THE SACRED HEART
ATTRIBUTED TO SAINT CLAUDE

My adorable Redeemer, I give and consecrate myself to thy Sacred Heart in the fullest and most complete way of which I am capable. I have, as it were, nailed myself to thy Cross by the vows of my profession. I renew them before heaven and earth in thy divine Heart and thank thee for having inspired me to take these vows. I acknowledge that the yoke of thy holy service is neither heavy nor burdensome and that I am not weighed down by my bonds. So far am I from wishing to be released from them that I would wish to multiply them and fasten the knots more closely.

Therefore I embrace the beloved cross of my vocation and will bear it till my death; it shall be all my joy, my glory, my delight. "God forbid that I should glory, save in the Cross of our Lord Jesus Christ, by whom the world is crucified to me, and I to the world" (Gal 6:14).

God forbid that I should ever have any other treasure than his poverty, any other joys than his sufferings, any other love than himself! My dearest Savior, I will never abandon thee; I will cling to none save thee; the narrowest paths of the perfect life to which I am called have no terrors for me, since thou art my light and my strength.

I hope, therefore, O my Lord, that thou wilt make me firm to resist all temptations, and victorious over the attacks of my enemies, and that thou wilt stretch out over me thy hand which has already bestowed so many favors upon me, so that I may be yet further enriched.

By thy Blood, by thy Wounds, and by thy Sacred Heart I implore thee, O adorable Jesus, to grant that by consecrating to thee all that I am, I may this day become a new work of thy love.

Amen.

Spiritual Notes. London, 1678

My Jesus, let me live in thy Heart and pour all my bitterness into it where it will be utterly consumed. Sheltered in thy Heart I shall not fear impatience. There I will practice silence, resignation to thy will, and constancy. I will thank thee daily for my crosses and ask thy pardon for those who offend me. I will try to acquire patience. I know it is not the work of a day, but it is enough for me to be sure that it can be attained by effort.

O my sweet Jesus, do thou pray for me as thou didst pray for thy enemies; do not refuse me this for I long to love thee and even to love my cross and my enemies for love of thee.

Amen.

Retreat Notes. London, 1677

O adorable Savior, vouchsafe to grant my desire to consecrate myself entirely to love and reparation to thy divine Heart and to accept the gift I make to thee of all that I am and all that I have. In reparation for all the outrages committed against thee and for the terrible ingratitude thou dost suffer from men, I consecrate to thee myself and my life. Give and take what thou wilt; use me or set me aside as a useless instrument; give me consolations or give me trials; may thy will be done in all things. May all this glorify thy divine Heart and make reparation to it. I wish to make a full gift of all this to thee, begging thee to accept it and to use it freely for the salvation of sinners.

Amen.

ON RECOLLECTION AND THE
PRESENCE OF GOD

Letter 128. London, 1678

You think you would be less distracted if you were away from the circumstances in which God has placed you; I think, on the contrary, that you would have fewer distractions if you accepted things with more conformity to God's will and if, in your work, you thought of yourself as a servant of Jesus Christ whom he employs as it seems best to him and who is equally content in whatever service is exacted from her. Try to live in your present state as though you were never to leave it; think more of making good use of your crosses than of getting rid of them under pretext of having more liberty with which to serve God.

Letter 126. London, 1678

Exterior employment is no obstacle to solitude of heart when the mind is calm and leaves everything in God's hands; when all that one does for others is done with humility and resignation; when we believe that nothing happens without God's permission; when we obey others as God himself; and when we persuade ourselves that their words, actions, temper, conduct, faults, everything in general and in particular, is ordained by the will of God, who knows all that is to happen and who allows and wills it for our good and his glory.

Retreat Notes. Lyons, 1674

The practice of the presence of God is very efficacious in leading us to contempt of worldly things. Saint Basil says that a man who has a king and a footman as witness of his actions does not think of the footman but only of gaining the approbation of his sovereign. It is an extraordinary and wretched servitude and slavery when a man only seeks to please other men. When shall I be able to say: "The world is crucified to me and I to the world" (Gal 6:14).

Retreat Notes. Lyons, 1674

I have promised with God's grace not to begin any action without remembering that he is witness of it—that he performs it together with me and gives me the means to do it; never to conclude any without the same thought, offering it to him as belonging to him, and in the course of the action whenever the same thought shall occur, to stop for a moment and renew the desire of pleasing him.

Retreat Notes. Lyons, 1674

God is in the midst of us, or rather we are in the midst
of him; wherever we are he sees us and touches us: at
prayer, at work, at table, at recreation. We do not think
of this; if we did, with what fervor and devotion we
should live. Let us often make acts of faith, saying to
ourselves: God is looking at me, he is here present.

Letter 138. London, 1678

Keep yourself as much as possible in the presence of
God, humbly tasting the sweetness you will find there.
Do not fear illusion. Despise troublesome thoughts and
bear their importunity with resignation. A soul that
fears God is not troubled by her fear of committing
faults; she goes to her good Master with great liberty of
spirit and with childlike confidence. When we only
desire to please him, we must not fear that he is offended
by things that we believe to be well done.

Letter 3. London, 1675–1676

How I should envy you your quiet place of retreat,
even with all your sufferings, if I were not quite sure
that there is no greater good upon earth than to do the
will of him who governs us. I know there is no work so
heavy that it need hinder a person who only undertakes

it for supernatural reasons and because God wishes it.
But it is certainly a difficulty to be perpetually among
men and to seek nothing but God, to have always two
or three things more to do than one can accomplish and
nevertheless to keep that peace of soul without which
we cannot possess God; to have hardly a moment to
enter into oneself and to recollect oneself in prayer, and
yet to keep a hold upon oneself. All this is possible, but
you must admit it is not easy. It is possible to be a saint
anywhere and everywhere when one really wishes to
become one.

Letter 100. London, 1677

The only secret for accomplishing your actions well is
to do them only to please God and to avoid anxiety and
discouragement at your faults: this comes merely from
self-love, because you think more of yourself than of
God; yet we should think only of him.

ON PERFECTION AND HOLINESS

Retreat Notes. Lyons, 1674

No matter what price I have to pay, God must be pleased with me.

Retreat Notes. Lyons, 1674

I see that we have to take many steps before arriving at sanctity. We think every step we take can be the last, and then we find that we have done nothing, we have hardly begun. A man who enters religion thinks there is nothing left to be done, but he soon finds that he has taken himself with him and is still worldly even though he has left the world. So he must go on another step and detach his heart from the world and from all created things.

It is one thing to leave the world and quite another to become a true religious. That done he must go a step further and detach himself from himself, seek only God in God, not look for any passing gain in holiness which would be a gross fault, but not even look for spiritual gain as such: to seek nothing but God's interests.

For this, my Lord, thou must give us a great grace,

for how can we reach such purity of intention by ourselves?

Spiritual Notes. Lyons, 1674

How I fear for my salvation when I see how inconstant I am. I am now gay, now sad: today I am friendly with everyone, tomorrow I am like a hedgehog that no one can touch without being pricked. This is a sign that nature still reigns within us, that our passions are still unmortified and that we have very little virtue. A man who leans on God is immovable and cannot be over-thrown. Whatever happens that is annoying, he is pleased because he has no other will than that of God. O happy peaceful state! but we must fight to obtain it.

Spiritual Notes. Lyons, 1674

As perfection consists in trying to please God in every-thing and to please him only, we must not hesitate when we get an opportunity of pleasing him and of being praised by him however much we displease men and lose their esteem.

Spiritual Notes. Lyons, 1674

When we consider God's greatness, we must realize what an honor it is to belong entirely to him. God confers an immense honor upon us in calling us to sanctity.

Supposing a king chose one of his subjects to be entirely at his service, so that he was not allowed to serve anyone else at all but was to enjoy the royal friendship, what an honor this would be. This has made me understand the favor of being called by God.

If God reigns in us, we shall obey his slightest commands and do nothing except by his orders. We shall try to please him in all things, to forestall his desires, to study his wishes and always do that which we think will please him most.

Spiritual Notes. Lyons, 1674

The grace of God is a seed that we must not stifle, but neither must we expose it too much. We must cherish it in our heart and not let it appear much to others.

Letter 49. Paray, 1682

It is God only who can sanctify us, and it is no small thing to desire sincerely that he may do all that is necessary for this, for of ourselves we have neither sufficient light nor sufficient strength.

ON CONFIDENCE IN GOD

Retreat Notes. Lyons, 1674

IN thinking of what could trouble me at death, that is to say past sin and future punishment, this thought came to me and I have made it my own; it is a great consolation to me: at death, when my sins known and unknown trouble me, I will take them all and cast them at Our Lord's feet to be consumed in the fire of his mercy. The greater they are, the worse they seem to me, the more willingly will I give them to him because the offering will be all the more worthy of his mercy. It seems to me that I could do nothing more reasonable nor more glorious to God, and because of the idea I have of his goodness, this will not be difficult. I feel greatly drawn to act in this way. As for purgatory, I do not fear it. I am sorry to have deserved it because it has only been by offending God; but since I do deserve it, I am glad to go there to satisfy his justice as rigorously as possible even to the day of judgment. I know the torments are great, but I know that they honor God and that in purgatory I shall be sure of never opposing God's will and of never complaining of the severity of his justice but of loving it and waiting patiently until it is entirely satisfied.

Retreat Notes. Lyons, 1674

God sought me out when I fled from him; he will not abandon me now that I seek him, or at least do not flee from him any more.

Letter 127. London, 1678

Cultivate thoughts of confidence as long as it pleases God to give them to you; they honor God far more than contrary thoughts. The more wretched we are, the more is God honored by the confidence we have in him. It seems to me that if your confidence were as great as it ought to be, you would not worry about what may happen to you; you would place it all in God's hands, hoping that when he wants something of you he will let you know what it is.

Letter 110. Paray, 1674

I do not know what you mean by despair: one would think you had never heard of God or of his infinite mercy. Hold such sentiments in horror, and remember that all you have done is nothing in comparison with your want of confidence. Hope on to the end.

Letter 22. London, 1676

Pray that my faults, however grave and frequent, may never make me despair of his goodness. That, in my opinion, would be the greatest evil that could befall anyone. When we can protect ourselves against that evil, there is no other which may not turn to our good and from which we cannot easily draw great advantage.

Letter 96. London, 1678

I was touched with sorrow in reading your letter, not so much for the faults you have committed as for the sad state into which they have thrown you because of the little confidence you have in God's goodness and in the loving ease with which, you ought to know, he receives back those who have offended him most grievously. I can see the wiles and malice of the devil who is trying to profit by your faults to throw you into despair, while on the other hand the Spirit of God would lead you to humility and compunction and inspire you to make reparation for what you have done. The evil is great, but it is not irremediable; it may even be a most valuable remedy to cure you entirely of all pride and presumption. If I were in your place, this is how I would console myself. I would say to God with great confidence: "Lord, here is a soul who exists only to show forth thy mercy in presence of heaven and earth.

Others glorify thee in showing the strength of thy grace by their fidelity and constancy, they show how liberal thou art to those who are faithful. As for me, I will glorify thee in showing how good thou art toward sinners, that thy mercy is above all malice and that nothing can exhaust it; that no fall, however shameful and guilty it be, should make the sinner despair of pardon. I have grievously offended thee, O my loving Lord, but it would be worse if I insulted thee by despairing of my pardon. In vain thine enemy and mine sets new snares for me: I will lose everything rather than the hope I have in thy mercy. If I had fallen a hundred times, and my sins were a hundred times worse than they are, I would still hope in thee."

After this it seems to me that nothing I could do in reparation for my sin and the scandal I had given would cost me too much. Then I would begin to serve God with more fervor than before and with as much peace as though I had never offended him.

Letter 75. London, 1678

What are you dreaming of to fear Our Lord has abandoned you! Will he, who has never abandoned you when you appeared to leave him, abandon you now that you seek him. Drive away the devil who suggests such things to you, it is a thought which outrages God's mercy, and do Our Lord the justice of believing him to be infinitely good, after all the proofs you have had of his infinite mercy.

Letter 72. London (date unknown)

Do you know what I should do if I were as near having to render my account as they tell me you are? I should excite my confidence by using the thought of the number and gravity of my sins. It shows a confidence really worthy of God when a person, far from being discouraged at the sight of her faults, strengthens herself on the contrary by the thought of the goodness of her Creator. It seems to me that confidence which rests on innocence and purity of life does not give such great glory to God. Is to save a holy soul who has never offended him all that the mercy of our God can do? It is certain that the confidence that honors Our Lord the most is that of a sinner who is so certain of the infinite mercy of God that all his sins seem to him but an atom in comparison.

Perhaps you will say that you have done nothing yet for heaven: that you have done no penance, acquired no holiness and no virtue. Well, even so, will that prevent the will of God from being accomplished? Is it not better that his will should be done rather than that we should attain to the holiness of Our Lady? These are the dispositions in which I hope you will render your soul into the hands of Our Lord Jesus Christ: namely, that even if you knew infallibly that by living a single day through your own will, you would go straight to heaven and be placed among the Seraphim, you would rather die by God's will and go to satisfy his justice in purgatory till the end of the world. Thy will be done, my God, that is the one thing necessary. That I die sooner or later, from one illness rather than from another, entirely purified or not, matters little provided that I die at the moment, from the illness, and in the state of perfection that pleases Our Lord. Try to attain to this spirit of a true victim: throw yourself blindly into the arms of God and trust that he will never allow a soul to be lost whose only confidence is in him, and who abandons herself to him without reserve.

Sermon preached in 1678

My God, I am so intimately convinced that thou dost watch over all those who hope in thee, and that we can want for nothing while we expect all from thee, that I am resolved to live without anxiety in the future, casting all my care on thee. "In peace I will sleep and I will rest for thou hast wonderfully established me in hope" (Ps 4:8). Men may turn against me: sickness may take away my strength and the means of serving thee; I may even lose thy grace by sin, but I will never lose my hope. I will keep it even to the last moment of my life, and all the demons in hell shall try in vain to tear it from me. In peace I will sleep and I will rest.

Others may look for happiness from their riches or their talents; they may rely upon the innocence of their lives, the rigor of their penance, the number of their good works, or the fervor of their prayers; but for me, O Lord, my confidence shall be my confidence itself. For thou hast wonderfully established me in hope.

This confidence has never deceived anyone. No one hath hoped in the Lord and been put to shame. I am sure that I shall be eternally happy, because I hope firmly to be so, and it is from thee, O Lord, that I hope it. In thee, O Lord, have I hoped; I shall not be confounded for ever.

I know that I am frail and changeable; I know the power of temptation against the most firmly based virtues: I have seen the stars of heaven and the pillars of the firmament fall; but not even this can make me fear. As long as I hope, I am safe from every evil, and I am sure of always hoping because I hope for this unchanging hope. For thou, O Lord, hast wonderfully established me in hope.

In fine, I am sure that I cannot hope too much in thee; and that I cannot obtain less than I hope for from thee. Thus I hope that thou wilt uphold me in the greatest dangers, protect me in the most violent assaults, and make my weakness triumph over my most formidable enemies. I hope that thou wilt love me always and that I also shall love thee with unfailing love; and to carry my hope at once as far as it can go, I hope for thee from thyself, my Creator, both in time and in eternity. Amen.

Retreat Notes. London, 1677

I am resolved to put no limit to my trust and to extend it to everything. It seems to me that I ought to make use of Our Lord as an armor which covers me all about, by means of which I shall resist every device of my enemies. Thou, then, shalt be my strength, O my God! Thou shalt be my guide, my director, my counsellor, my patience, my knowledge, my peace, my justice, and my prudence. I will have recourse to thee in my temptations, in my dryness, in my repugnances, in my weariness, in my fears; or rather I will no longer fear either the illusions or the tricks of the demon, nor my own weakness, my indiscretions, nor even my mistrust of myself. For thou must be my strength in all my crosses. Thou dost promise me that this thou wilt be in proportion to my confidence. And wonderful indeed it is. O my God, that at the same time that thou imposest this condition, it seems to me that thou givest me the confidence wherewith to fulfill it. Mayest thou be eternally loved and praised by all creatures. O my very loving Lord! If thou wert not my Strength, alas, what should I do? But since thou art, and since thou dost assure me that thou art, what shall I not do for thy glory? "Omnia possum in eo qui me confortat" (Phil 4:13).

Thou art everywhere in me and I in thee; therefore in whatever situation I may find myself, in whatever peril, whatever enemy may rise up against me, I have my support always with me. This thought alone can, in a moment, scatter all my trials, especially those uprisings of nature which at times I feel so strong and which in spite of myself make me fear for my perseverance and tremble at the sight of the perfect emptiness in which it has pleased God to place me.

ON ABANDONMENT TO
GOD'S WILL

Retreat Notes. Lyons, 1674

I AM resigned to sanctify myself in the way and by the means God wants me to sanctify myself: without any sensible sweetness if he so wills; by interior trial and by continual struggle against my passions: all this seems the hardest thing in life for me, yet I submit with all my heart and all the more willingly because I know it is the surest way, the way least subject to illusion and the shortest for acquiring perfect purity of heart, great love of God, and great merit.

Sermon

Submission to God's will frees us from all other yokes. Because as God wills everything that happens to us, and as we will all that God wills, nothing can happen except what we will. Nobody can oblige me to do what I do not want to do because I desire to do all that God wishes. A lady, having been asked if during the danger she encountered on her journey she had not hoped that God would protect her, replied No, but that she had hoped that he would do what was most for his glory and that in this dependence upon the divine will she was always calm and happy.

Letter 138. London, 1678

By the sickness he sends you, God asks of you great contempt for all things, great indifference about life and death, perfect abandonment to his divine will, a sovereign and infinite respect for this adorable will which you must prefer to everything else and in which you must find your pleasure, and also a great love of the cross, especially of all that humiliates body and mind.

Spiritual Notes. Lyons, 1674

Our Lord requires a great sacrifice of me, and that is to make up my mind to do nothing if it is his will. I must be ready to die and to sacrifice in death my zeal and the great desire I have to work for the sanctification of souls; or I must be ready to live on in silence, weak and ill, being no more than a burden wherever I find myself.

Spiritual Notes. Lyons, 1674

Since I have been ill I have learned that we cling to ourselves with many imperceptible threads, and if God did not free us from them we should never do so ourselves: we do not even see them. Illness was a thing absolutely necessary for me; without it I do not know what I should have become. I am sure it is one of the greatest mercies God has shown me. If I had only profited by it, it would have sanctified me.

ON TEMPTATIONS

Letter 13. S. Symphorien d'Ozon, 1679

BE on your guard against the first movements of passion, especially of the love of pleasure and honor. Love of pleasure includes friendships. Unless I am mistaken, you are very impressionable on this point, and it is hardly in your power to control these passions once you have let them enter your heart. First of all they occupy your attention; then they take up your time and application and make you neglect everything else, so that in the end, when they begin to die down, you feel lost, so to speak, so far away from God. You have strayed off the right path and not knowing how to find your way you are in danger of wandering in any direction to which nature calls you. This is why you must fight against the first movements of passion and prevent them if possible by great recollection.

Letter 77. London, 1678

If you fall under the stress of temptation, rise promptly, ask God's pardon, hope in him in spite of your fall, and with all your heart welcome the humiliation and detest the sin. Your uncertainty as to whether you sin or not is another cross that you must also bear with perfect resignation.

Letter 98. London, 1678

Do not torment yourself about getting rid of thoughts that assail you; all the resistance you should make, you do make in humbling yourself under the mighty hand of God's justice which strikes you and in willingly accepting all that it pleases him to send you. You do not consent to these imaginations, but even if you fell under the strength of the temptation, you must rise courageously and hate the sin with all your heart. I do not advise you to confess these things. If you like you can say in general that you have had all sorts of thoughts, some of them very bad in themselves, but that you do not think they were voluntary. Courage, my child, bear what Our Lord sends you with submission and love. Place yourself on his side and be glad to see him chastising you in proportion to your sins. Try to please him by perfect acceptance of the severest measures of his justice, and this by willingly accepting all that happens, all that is humiliating to body and soul, and especially your confusion and repentance at having used a life so badly that you might have employed so usefully. Let your compunction be mingled with a certain pleasure at the sight of yourself: poor, miserable, humbled, deprived of all merit and virtue.

Letter 136. London, 1677

Despise temptations against faith and remember that you believe what so many saints and doctors of the Church have believed. Be ashamed of your fear of the future. Do you not know that your heavenly Father knows your needs and is all-powerful to provide for them? What do you fear in God's judgments? They are always favorable to souls of good will.

ON PEACE DURING INTERIOR TRIALS

Retreat Notes. Lyons, 1674

THERE is no peace except in perfect forgetfulness of self; we must resolve to forget even our spiritual interests, so that we may seek nothing but God's glory.

Retreat Notes. Lyons, 1674

In meditating on Jesus being taken prisoner in the Garden, two things touched me very much and occupied my thoughts: first the way Christ went forward to meet those who had come to apprehend him: his firmness, courage, and peace just as if his soul had been steeped in calm. His Heart is full of anguish, his human nature is disconcerted, yet amidst it all it turns straight to God the Father; it does not hesitate about taking the way suggested by the highest virtue and self-sacrifice.

One of the greatest gifts the Holy Spirit can bestow on us is to give us peace in time of struggle, calm in the midst of trouble, so that in time of desolation we are armed with so virile a courage that nature, the devil, and even God himself, who seems to be against us, cannot withstand.

The second thing that struck me was Our Lord's dispositions with regard to Judas who betrayed him, to the apostles who abandoned him, and to the priests and others who were the cause of the persecution he suffered. Amidst it all Jesus remained perfectly calm, his love for his disciples and enemies was not altered at all; he grieved over the harm they did themselves, but his own sufferings, far from troubling him, comforted him because he knew they would act as a remedy for the sins of his enemies. His Heart was without bitterness and full of tenderness toward his enemies in spite of their perfidy and of all they made him suffer.

Spiritual Reflections

I feel more wretched than I can say: my imagination is foolish and extravagant. All my passions rise in me, hardly a day passes without my being tempted to give way to them. Sometimes real and sometimes imaginary things excite them. By God's grace I suffer all this without consenting to them, yet I am continually troubled by these foolish passions. Self-love hides everywhere; I am very sorry for myself, but I am not vexed or impatient, what would be the good? I pray that I may know what I ought to do to please and serve God and purify myself; but I am resolved to wait peacefully until he works this miracle in me, for I am convinced he alone can do it.

Letter 95. London, 1678

I see that you have at last found the secret of true peace: not to examine your present state and to abandon the past and future entirely to God's mercy; to have a great idea of his goodness, which is infinitely greater than you can express, and to believe, in spite of anything that tries to persuade you to the contrary, that you are loved by him in spite of all your miseries. Guard these thoughts preciously; they are most certainly from God.

Letter 93. Lyons, 1679

The trouble into which your dissipation and distractions throw you, your sense of separation from God and all your resistance to what is good would cease if you received these painful states humbly; they are neither sins nor spiritual evils, but merely the loving chastisement of your Father, who uses this way of purifying you from all the stains of your former life. All that saddens you and makes you think you are lost will, if borne with patience, humility, and conformity to God's will, be changed into a treasure which will enrich you more in one day than would a whole year of consolation and ecstasies.

Letter 117. London, 1678

Never doubt that God will give you all that is necessary
for you, for he never allows a soul to perish who would
rather perish than offend him. I confess that I cannot
forgive a servant of Jesus Christ who is troubled and
anxious even for a moment. If you are troubled, you
wrong your good Master who bears with, preserves,
and fills with his gifts even his greatest enemies; so you
may judge if he would be willing to lose those who
think only of serving him.

Letter 116. Paray, 1675

You fear that God may send you trials you are not able
to bear; that is a mere passing thought; if I thought you
really entertained it, I should not easily forgive you for
this want of confidence and for the insult you offer to
the wisdom and goodness of Our Lord. You cannot
sufficiently impress upon your mind that it is he who
does everything in us, our sins excepted, so that we
must think neither of our faults nor of our weakness,
but hope for everything from him alone.

Letter 138. London, 1678

All that troubles you must be despised. You must bear
the incertitude you are in of being pleasing to God and

resist all worrying thoughts; suffer it all with patience and resignation, and throw yourself into the arms of him who knows all and who loves you. Say to him: My God, however it be, I love thee with all my heart and wish I had never offended thee.

Letter 140. London, 1678

Love in the darkness and uncertainty in which God wishes you to be: What does it matter where the love comes from, provided it be followed by good results?

Letter 136. London, 1678

How foolish to wonder if your troubles come from God! Where else could they come from? Does anything on earth happen without his order or permission? So then, whether your trouble comes from the devil, as did that of Job, or from your own corrupt nature, as happens to so many holy souls, are they for that reason less precious?

Letter 3. London, 1676

I do not know if your troubles continue, but I know very well that to a heart that is pure and detached from creatures there is no suffering that prevents it from being united to its Creator.

Letter 67. Lyons, 1681

God is touched by our sorrows and does not allow them to last for ever. He takes pleasure in trying our love for a time because he sees that trials purify us and render us worthy to receive his greater graces; but he considers our weakness, and one would even think that he suffered with us, so anxious is he to relieve us. May he be eternally blessed and praised by all his creatures.

Letter 103. London, 1677

In Our Lord's name I beg of you to live in peace and to allow no trouble to upset you. We wrong Our Lord when we allow ourselves a single moment of distrust. We have a remedy for all our evils in his goodness; I see more and more that if our trouble comes from ourselves, a little courage and mortification gives back peace to the most troubled souls.

Letter 74. London, 1677

You will never be troubled except by a bad spirit and through lack of virtue. True virtue animates, encourages, and always urges us to advance; it thinks it has done nothing and it is right; but it does not lose its interior peace on that account. Any suggestion which troubles the soul or weakens its hope of acquiring holiness is infallibly from the devil.

Letter 55. Lyons, 1680

Love thrives on suffering; and suffering is to be found everywhere.

Letter 63. Lyons, 1679

No plans we make for God are ever accomplished without trouble. The more the devil tries to upset them, the more glory for God can we hope for.

Retreat Notes. Lyons, 1674

The time of desolation and dryness is the best for gaining merit. A soul that seeks God easily bears this state and rises above all that passes before the imagination and in the inferior part of the soul where consolation is mostly to be found. It does not cease to love God, to humble itself, and to accept this state even for ever. There is nothing so dangerous and so much to be suspected as sweetness. Sometimes we attach ourselves to it, and when it is passed we find we have less instead of more fervor in doing good. It is a real consolation for me to think that in the midst of aridity and temptation my heart is free and that it is only by my heart (that is, my will) that I can merit or demerit; that I neither please nor displease God by things which are beyond my control, such as sensible sweetness and importunate thoughts which come into my mind in spite of myself.

Therefore during this time of suffering and desolation I say to God: My Lord, let the world and even the devil take for themselves what I cannot prevent them having, but they shall never have anything to do with my heart, my will that thou hast left in my possession — this belongs to thee: take it, it is thine, and do what thou wilt with it. A man to whom God has given a real desire to please him need never trouble about anything. "Peace to men of good will" (Lk 2:14).

Retreat Notes. Lyons, 1674

I am not much astonished at the injustice of Pilate in condemning Jesus, but what touches me is to see Jesus Christ submitting to so unjust a sentence; to see him taking up his Cross with such wonderful humility, meekness, and resignation; to look at him on Calvary allowing himself to be stripped and stretched upon the Cross, offering his hands and feet to be nailed and offering himself to his Father as he alone could. This makes me love the Cross; without it I do not think I could be happy. I look with reverence on those whom God visits with humiliation and adversities of whatever kind they may be. No doubt they are his favorites. To humble myself I have only to compare myself with them as long as things go well with me.

ON FERVOR

Retreat Notes. Lyons, 1674

IT is strange how many enemies we have to fight as soon as we make the resolution to become a saint. It would seem that everything is let loose against us: the devil with his snares; the world and its attractions; nature with its resistance to all good desires; the praise of the good; the mockery of the wicked; the suggestions of the tepid. If God visits us, vanity is to be feared. If God withdraws himself, we fall into dejection. Despair may succeed the greatest fervor.

Our friends tempt us because we are accustomed to try and please them; the indifferent because we fear to displease them. Indiscretion is to be feared in fervor, sensuality in moderation, and self-love everywhere. What is to be done? We have no refuge but in thee, O God. "As we know not what to do, we can only turn our eyes to thee" (2 Chron 20:12).

Above all, as sanctity does not consist in being faithful for a day or a year but in persevering until death, we must use God as a shield which covers us completely because we are attacked from all sides. "His truth shall compass thee as a shield" (Ps 91:5).

God must do everything. All the better; there will be no fear of failure. As for ourselves, we have only to acknowledge our powerlessness and to be fervent and constant in asking for help through the intercession of Mary, to whom God refuses nothing; but even this we cannot do without a great grace, or rather without many graces.

Letter 137. London, 1678

The spirit of God inclines us to fervor, but this fervor is calm and causes no trouble either to ourselves or to others; when it meets with obstacles it knows how to stop and submit to God's will. Its only arms are patience and gentleness. You want to be a martyr; you have a daily martyrdom which you endure unwillingly and without resignation! I see nothing reasonable in such a desire and nothing which looks like an inspiration.

ON THE LOVE OF OUR NEIGHBOR

SOMETIMES we see souls who worry because they feel no love of God, are cold at prayer, and have not even a spark of the fervor which the saints had. Then they begin to doubt if they are in the state of grace and if God loves them, seeing that they love him so little. Be comforted. You have more love of God than you think. Not only do you wish evil to no one, but you wish them well; you do as much good as you can to all. You do not know what it is to take revenge; far from grieving over your neighbor's prosperity, you rejoice in his good fortune: in one word—you love others. Therefore do not doubt that you love God. These two loves cannot be separated. It is impossible to have one without the other.

I have often pondered with joy and admiration over the extreme care Jesus took to urge us to love others. In the Gospel we read that he commanded it above all things. "Love one another as I have loved you. . . . By this shall

all men know that you are my disciples if you have love one for another" (Jn 13:34, 35). Another time he tells us that no reason either of interest or of honor allows us to hate another; he will not acknowledge us and he ranks us with pagans and infidels if we do not love our enemies, if we will not pray for them and serve them when occasion offers. In fact, it seems as though the whole Christian code were reduced to this point. It is the summing up of all the commandments. Saint Paul tells us this: "Love is the fulfilling of the law" (Rom 13:10).

My God, how sweet and humane this commandment seems! How worthy of the goodness and wisdom of God! It is but reasonable that men who have the same nature, the same religion, the same Father, men who are obliged to live together, who are fellow-travellers, and who are to be together for all eternity in heaven, should begin to love each other here and should render each other mutual services such as they would wish themselves to receive.

My Lord, does not thy zeal for charity go too far when thou dost tell us to leave our offering to our Creator and go and be reconciled with our enemy? Ought not the service of God to be preferred before everything else? Is not our obligation to honor him who made us greater than that of being re-united to one who perhaps dishonors thee? Wilt thou not allow us to fulfill our duty toward thee from whom we have received so many benefits and then be civil to those who offend us? No. Jesus Christ wishes us to begin with our enemies, and then come and offer our sacrifice to him: "Go first to be reconciled to thy brother, and then coming thou shalt offer thy gift" (Mt 5:24).

Spiritual Reflections

Love of pleasure is sacrificed when we refrain from revenge and spite, for of all pleasures, revenge is perhaps the one which flatters nature most. There is nothing so pleasing to nature as to see those who hate us humiliated and forced to repent of the harm they have done us. This is why vindictive and revengeful people not only want to harm their enemy but want him to know who does the harm, so that they can rejoice in the pain they give him. Saint Augustine says that such conduct acts as a balm to soothe the wound they have received. Therefore a man who takes no revenge when he could, deprives himself of a great pleasure and suffers pain for God's sake when he might either lessen or even assuage it altogether.

Revenge does not consist in killing or fighting and such things, these can be done from a motive of justice. To take revenge is to rejoice at the misfortune of another, to find pleasure and consolation in anything that hurts or afflicts our enemy, whether this affliction comes from ourselves or from others.

Now it is a fact that few persons are quite exempt from these feelings, and it is not easy to overcome them.

Retreat Notes. Lyons, 1674

To consider the virtues of others makes charitable people rejoice that they have these virtues and that God is glorified by them. Charity "rejoiceth not in iniquity, but rejoiceth in the truth" (1 Cor 13:6). Do we so rejoice? We should praise God and thank him, asking him to give them grace to persevere in virtue. This is the way to share in the good works of others. Sometimes we may even gain more than they, because of our disinterestedness. Saint Augustine says: If you are jealous because your brother is more mortified than you, rejoice in his virtue, and then it belongs to you.

No, my God, I am not jealous of the virtues of others. On the contrary, I humble myself and am ashamed when I compare them with myself. There are few in whom I do not find excellent qualities which I do not possess. It may be that they have their faults, but they are mostly involuntary; and a sinner like myself ought hardly to notice them and always to excuse them, looking at my own faults. Their virtue is generally true virtue. Thus should we keep our souls in humility, in reverence, and in charity. Do I do this? No; and it is a sign of my pride. Instead of this jealousy, O my God, enkindle in me a holy desire to imitate the virtues of others and to profit by their example. At the day of judgment they will condemn me; today they should urge me on and encourage me. They are helps that God gives me. The example of the saints of old should touch us less than that given us by those around us whom we see daily: I see their self-control in spite of their hasty temperament, their humility in spite of their high-birth, their mortification and austerity in spite of their delicate health. What a disgrace it would be for me to have such great examples of virtue before my eyes and not to profit by them.

Retreat Notes. Lyons, 1674

God is in the midst of us, and it seems that we do not recognize him. He is in our neighbor and desires to be served, loved, and honored in him, and he will reward us more than if we served him in person. How do I behave toward my neighbor? How toward my brothers? If I except a single one, it is not Jesus Christ I consider in them. I do not recognize him in them. If I love them, it is merely so that I may be liked and considered, or because their character suits mine.

Let each one see Jesus Christ in his neighbor.

Letter 89. London, 1678

As for feelings of resentment, I can only say one thing: anything which is not voluntary is not sin, and great charity may exist simultaneously with strong indeliberate feelings of hatred and revenge. All that is required is that in spite of them you do not give up praying for the people for whom you feel an aversion; that you speak and act toward them as if you liked them, and that in the depths of your heart you desire to have all the charity that God wishes those who really love him to have.

ON FAITH

Spiritual Reflections

IT is an error to think that faith is so entirely a gift of God that it is not in our power to increase and strengthen it. Some admit that they have very little faith and excuse themselves on this account for their bad lives. Therefore when they are reproached for having so little faith, it makes no more impression upon them than if you told them they had not the gift of miracles. They admire faith in the saints as a purely gratuitous grace; they persuade themselves that they can do nothing to increase their own faith and that the only thing to do is to remain passive until God grants them that favor; they will make no effort to grow in faith, saying that to do so is quite useless. "I know my faith is weak," they say, "but it is no good me trying to rekindle it; I cannot do it. I wish I were like those saints who without any trouble were detached from everything but God. What is the good of me wishing for these things if God does not intend to give them to me?"

We must get rid of these ideas, see why it is our faith is so weak, and acknowledge that it is our own fault and that, whatever we may say, the truth is that we do not believe because we do not wish to believe.

Of all states to be in, the most wretched is that of a Christian who has but little faith. It would be better to have none because such a one suffers more even in his pleasures than a man of real faith does in the greatest trials: the little he possesses is enough to damn him but not enough to save him. To him faith is like a light which disturbs the rest one finds in darkness and not like the light which brings the joy of day.

ON SPIRITUAL JOY

Retreat Notes, Lyons, 1674

By God's infinite mercy I feel a liberty of spirit which fills me with great joy. It seems as though nothing could now make me unhappy. The thought that I am serving God fills me with this joy, and I feel that it is of far greater value than all the favor of kings would be. The occupations of the worldly seem very despicable in comparison with work done for God.

Retreat Notes. Lyons, 1674

I know no greater joy than to discover some weakness in myself that I did not realize before. I often taste this joy and shall always have it when God gives me his light when I am examining my conscience. I firmly believe, and in this I find joy, that God guides those who give themselves up to his leading and that he takes care of the least things that concern them.

Letter 74. London, 1677

We must serve God with our whole heart and do all in our power to prevent ourselves from sinning, but all this is to be done with joy, liberty of heart, and entire confidence, in spite of all the weakness that we feel and the faults we commit.

ON ZEAL

WE have a hundred opportunities of speaking of God which often succeed much better than a sermon. No one spoke to John Berchmans without being the better for it. Let us cultivate this zeal for souls. What do we generally talk about? If I speak little of thee, O my God, it is because I think seldom of thee and love thee too little.

It seems to me that I would give the last drop of my blood to save a soul from hell! How happy I should be if at death I could say to Our Lord: Thou didst shed thy Blood for the conversion of sinners, and I prevented it from being useless in such or such a case.

But what shall I say of myself if, while trying to convert others, I do not convert myself? Am I going to work to fill heaven and let myself be condemned to hell?

Spiritual Notes. Lyons, 1674

O loving God, how wonderful it would be if some day thou shouldst use my weakness to withdraw a soul from sin! If all that is required is my will, I give it to thee with all my heart. It is true that one must be holy in order to make others holy, and my great faults show me how far I am from sanctity. Make me holy, O my God, and do not spare me in the making, for I want to become a saint whatever it costs.

Retreat Notes. Lyons, 1674

An apostle is not called to a soft and easy life. He must be ready for fatigue and fear neither heat nor cold, nor fasting, nor watching. He must use his whole strength for his work. The worst that could happen would be for him to die while serving God and his neighbor, and I do not see that anyone need be afraid of this. Health and life ought to be indifferent to us, but sickness and death brought on by work for souls ought to be pleasing and precious to us.

Retreat Notes. Lyons, 1674

Jesus Christ chose poor, ignorant people for his apostles, people who from a human point of view were very ill-fitted for the work. Not that we must be ignorant and of low birth so as to work for souls, but to teach us how little natural or acquired talent counts and that it is never the cause of success. Christ chose fishermen to show us that it is not easy work; we have to be ready for great difficulties and fatigue.

Retreat Notes. Lyons, 1674

What a wonderful thought it is that Jesus Christ, who was able to convert the whole world by himself, should have chosen to do it through his disciples. He spent his whole life training them. Jesus took for himself what was difficult: an ignominious death, and left the renown to his disciples. What love Christ showed in allowing others to help him in work he could have done alone.

Retreat Notes. Lyons, 1674

A man called to convert others has need of great virtue, especially humility and obedience. We must not miss our opportunities but so turn things that we appear to be following advice rather than giving it and seem to be the instrument rather than the worker. This will humble us and make the work easier.

Retreat Notes. Lyons, 1674

We should honor all those who work for the salvation of souls and rejoice in their success. To act otherwise is ridiculous, most imperfect, very vain, and very far from the spirit of God.

Retreat Notes. Lyons, 1674

The apostolic life requires great mortification. Without it God does not enlighten us and we do not help our neighbor. A man who gives up his own ease and pleasure and who strives to subdue his passions speaks with far greater authority and makes a far deeper impression than an unmortified man.

Retreat Notes. Lyons, 1674

You are right in envying me my opportunities of urging others to love God; but you know that one's heart should be full of love so that it may overflow on those to whom one speaks. The sins of the man whom God uses as an instrument are a great obstacle to his designs.

From the moment we feel inspired by God to work for the sanctification of a soul, to the time when we have placed that soul in a certain degree of safety, there are many trials to be gone through. It is true there are also great consolations, especially in seeing the working of grace and its progress in the heart, in admiring the goodness of God, his patience, tenderness, and prudence, his power and a hundred other things which console those who reflect upon them. These things fill both heart and soul with joy.

Letter 35. London, 1678

You are happy in being chosen by God to enkindle his love in the hearts of others. To do this it is necessary to have deep humility and an entire distrust of self, besides zeal. We must act without haste and wait with peace and confidence until it pleases God to accomplish in these souls that which his grace alone is capable of doing and of which he alone must reap the glory.

ON HUMILITY AND SIMPLICITY

Letter 47. Lyons, 1679

ANYONE who thinks of what he is, what he has been, and what he can do of himself will find it difficult to be proud. To shatter pride it is enough to remember that the first sign of real virtue is to consider self as nothing at all. We have only to look at Jesus Christ who emptying himself gave all glory to his Father.

If people praise me, it is a mistake, an injustice done to God. People do not think so highly of us as we imagine: they know our faults, even those we do not see ourselves.

If God uses me for great things, he should be praised and thanked for making use of such a poor instrument, but I myself am not on that account any better; it might even happen that I shall be damned after having helped to save others.

We should imitate Our Lady: she acknowledged that God had done great things for her and that all generations would call her blessed, but instead of attributing anything to herself she says: "Magnificat anima mea Dominum" (Lk 1:46).

Retreat Notes. Lyons, 1674

It seems to me that a man who sees himself praised for some virtue or good action should be as ashamed as an honorable man would be to be taken for someone else and praised for things he had not done. If we are vain enough to be proud of our natural and supernatural qualities which do not belong to us, think of our shame and confusion on the day of judgment when before all men God will show all that he has given us and what we are of ourselves, reproaching us for our pride: "What hast thou that thou hast not received? and if thou hast received, why dost thou glory?" (1 Cor 4:7).

Retreat Notes. Lyons, 1674

I have in me the seeds of every vice: there is not one that I am not capable of committing. Only the grace of God prevents me from falling into the abyss. How humiliating this is! It is a thought that should make even the holiest souls ashamed.

Retreat Notes. Lyons, 1674

Really humble people are never scandalized: they know their own weakness too well; they know that they themselves are so close to the edge of the precipice and they are so afraid of falling over that they are not at all astonished to see others do so.

Spiritual Notes. Lyons, 1674

We have no reason to despise anyone. A humble man sees only his own faults. It is a sign of little virtue to notice the imperfections of others. A person may be imperfect today who in a little while, recognizing this, may rise to great sanctity.

Retreat Notes. London, 1677

It is very necessary to walk with great circumspection, humility, and distrust of self in directing others and in one's own spiritual life. We must be detached from our natural desire to make great progress; that leads to illusions and may make us indiscreet. Love of humility and abjection and a hidden and obscure life are the great remedies.

We compare ourselves unconsciously but quite ridiculously to the greatest saints and attempt to do through self-love what they did under the inspiration of the Holy Spirit. We want to accomplish in a day, both in ourselves and in others, what cost the saints many years of effort, yet we have neither their prudence, nor their experience, nor yet their talents and their supernatural gifts; in one word they were saints and we are not. But we are presumptuous enough to think we can do all that they did.

Letter 52. Paray, 1675

Once God is master of a heart, he does not remain idle. If you saw that you always remained the same, it would not be a good sign even though things seemed to be going on fairly well. When the world is entirely satisfied and even in admiration, a soul that is really enlightened from above finds a hundred things still with which to reproach itself and can only wonder at those who admire its virtue. I do not think there are any souls in the world with whom God is less pleased than with those who imagine they have reason to be pleased with themselves. As soon as we begin to see how lovable Our Lord is, we should have very hard hearts if we did not love him greatly; and when we love greatly, we think we have never done enough for him.

Letter 76. London, 1678

You must overcome everything by humility and simplicity. These virtues are not, as some think, the virtues of stupid people: on the contrary, stupid people are not capable of practicing them. We require a great deal of light to know ourselves and much strength to despise all that is not God so as to abandon ourselves to him and to those who govern us in his name. People who are less docile and who count on themselves because they think they know better are really greatly to be pitied. It would be a strange blindness to think there is any knowledge or prudence above the knowledge and prudence of God, so that we could be dispensed from following the teaching of the Gospel.

As for myself, I confess that the more sense I get, the more stupid seems to me that confidence in myself of which I had only too much. The more light I get by experience and self-study, the easier I find it to be humble and to practice that admirable simplicity which renounces its own views and interests so as to obey God and men.

I may be wrong, but after having closely examined the thing, it seems to me that all wisdom is enclosed in these two virtues. Once you have entered into the true practice of them, you are no longer subject to inconstancy but are, as it were, invulnerable; you enjoy such peace and tranquillity that nothing can disturb you; you are always satisfied and find consolation in everything; you become a real philosopher, which is a thing the greatest intellects among the pagans have aspired to but which only the disciples of the cross can claim with justice.

What an excellent proof it is of intelligence and of a great and noble mind to hold oneself of little account and to renounce one's own judgment, which always deceives us, however clever we be!

Letter 104. London, 1678

There is no true virtue without simplicity and humility. Simplicity makes us forget our own lights, and humility persuades us that everyone has more light than we. A really humble person sees only her own faults and not those of others. What a wretched occupation it is to be always examining what others do! Let us prefer rather to be blind and without judgment than to use our powers to consider and judge the actions of our neighbor. A heart that is full of the love of God occupies itself quite differently; it only thinks of suffering for him whom it loves, and it loves all those who give it an opportunity of suffering for its Beloved.

Beware of listening to the murmuring of others. Pay attention to yourself, and you will see that you will live far more happily and that God will dwell in you and find his delight in you.

Letter 148. Paray, 1681

If you want to be perfectly pleasing to him whom you love, you must take pleasure in your own extreme misery and love the nothingness in which God leaves you. He allows it on purpose the better to show forth his mercy by the patience with which he bears with you and by the graces he never ceases to give you. O child of little faith! Why do you doubt? Think only of abandoning yourself to the Providence of your tender Father, and live from day to day.

Spiritual Notes. Lyons, 1674

Open my eyes, O loving Jesus: "Lord, that I may see" (Lk 18:41). I do not ask now to see thee and know thee: give me light to know myself as I am, for if I know myself, I shall know thee: "Noverim me, noverim te" (Saint Augustine). I cannot know myself without knowing thee. My imperfections will give me a great desire of knowing something better than creatures, and that can only be the Creator. "All my desire is before thee" (Ps 37:9). Everything else displeases me and myself more than all the rest, for I know nothing more despicable and wretched.

ON DETACHMENT

THE thought of the greatness of God and of the nothingness of all created things has made me understand the foolishness of those who make themselves dependent upon other people and the happiness of those who depend only upon God.

There is only one way of raising ourselves above our own nothingness, and that is to cling to God: "He who is joined to the Lord is one spirit" (1 Cor 6:17). By doing this we rise above the things of earth and become in some measure like unto God.

One great means of detaching our heart from earthly things is to change our employment often: we become attached unconsciously and take root as we easily see by the difficulty we have in changing our usual customs. To have to leave a place where we are known and have friends is like a kind of death. A thought that will help us to bear these separations bravely is that God goes with me everywhere: I shall find the same Lord where I am going as I have here; from this point of view, there is no separation. I shall find the same God there as I pray to here, the same God who knows me, loves me, and whom I long to love.

Retreat Notes. London, 1677

There is no peace except in perfect forgetfulness of self. We must make up our mind to forget even our spiritual interests and think only of God's glory.

Retreat Notes. Lyons, 1674

Thinking of the eternity of God, I imagined it as an immovable rock on the bank of a river past which God sees every creature go by without ever moving himself. Those who are attached to created things appeared to me like people caught in the current, some clinging to a plank, others to the trunk of a tree, others to a mere heap of foam which they mistake for something solid. Everything is washed away by the torrent: friends die, health is shattered, life passes, and we arrive at eternity borne along by these passing props and plunge into it as we do into a sea which we cannot prevent ourselves from entering and where we perish.

Then we see how imprudent we have been not to attach ourselves to the immovable and eternal Rock; we would like to go back, but the waves have carried us on too far; we cannot return but must necessarily perish with all perishable things.

On the other hand, a man who clings to God sees the peril and loss of others without fear for himself; whatever happens he stands upon the rock. God cannot forsake him; he has clung to him alone and finds himself always upheld by the Eternal. Adversity comes and shows him what a good choice he has made. Such a man always possesses God; the death of his relations and friends, separation from all who esteem and favor him, distance, change of employment or of dwelling, age, sickness, or death, none of these things separate him from God. He is always happy and says in peace and joy of heart: "It is good for me to hold fast unto my God: to put my hope in the Lord God" (Ps 73:28).

Letter 13. S. Symphorien d'Ozon, 1679

It is such a great good to possess nothing but God and to be deprived of all the pleasures that we can taste . . . that we ought to consider all loss an advantage that places us in this state.

Letter 141. London, 1678

You ask me to what you must avoid becoming attached: You must be attached to nothing, neither fortune, nor relations, nor directors, nor interior consolation; there must be nothing in the world which we are not ready to forgo without trouble if God asks it of us.

ON VANITY AND VAINGLORY

Spiritual Notes. Lyons, 1674

I have resolved never to hesitate when an opportunity presents itself of humbling myself and of letting people see me as I am and know me as I have been. This will not be difficult if God gives me the grace to remember that the less we are esteemed by men, the more we are esteemed by God, and it is he alone I desire to please.

Retreat Notes. Lyons, 1674

I have noticed that when we are very careful to mortify and humble ourselves in everything, we sometimes become depressed and less ready to serve God. This is a temptation which we can conquer by thinking that God only asks these things of us through love. We should aim at humbling ourselves to please God as a good friend tries to please his friend, or a son his father. There must be no constraint but a holy liberty of spirit, for this liberty is one of the best signs of true love. It is easy to do things which we know will please one whom we love.

Spiritual Reflections

The world is like a troop of children who hardly know how to distinguish between good and evil. It is like a confused mass of people differing in character and tastes, most of whom have neither learning, nor virtue, nor judgment. One is blinded by pride, another by avarice; ambition has turned the head of one, and lust has changed another into a mere beast; hardly anyone has much common sense, yet all think themselves wise and capable of ruling others although they cannot govern themselves.

A woman who gets into her head the idea of making herself liked and admired lives in continual constraint: she will do and suffer anything to preserve the beauty she thinks she possesses and which she considers necessary for her plans. For this she has to take precautions at all times and seasons; she must put up with much that is painful, much that goes against her own inclinations and pleasure. Dressing is a regular business! It takes her four or five hours. She will go through tortures that body, head, and hair may be decked according to the fashion. She never passes her time worse than when in society, for she thinks of nothing else but of how she can attract notice by her words and actions. Please she must: but this person will be annoyed if she is too serious, and another if she is too gay. She must pretend to a gentleness that is foreign to her and to a wit which she does not possess. She is like a machine which must be wound up to please all tastes. Voice, lips, eyes, gestures—everything must be regulated. She certainly has plenty to do, and we can hardly be surprised if all this does away with any pleasure or freedom she might have enjoyed. If you could only know what she feels when she gets home after an evening for which she had prepared so long beforehand and upon which her hopes had rested. Things have not gone at all as she had hoped: she has not danced as often as she expected; she was not in the humor to talk; people did not laugh at her jokes; she made some tactless remarks; she expected to get more consideration from others, more kindness from a few; someone else seems to have attracted all the notice. All this bitterness is carried home, and even the servants remark it.

A single look, a good thought, a holy desire is enough to gain the Heart of God and the admiration of the heavenly hosts: "Thou hast wounded my Heart with one of thy eyes, with one hair of thy neck" (Song 4:9). But to be loved and considered by the world requires far more care and fatigue!

Do you want to know what you gain from those you try to please? Consider what they gain from you. You are not the only one thirsting for vainglory: nearly everyone runs after the same phantom. Confess that if you had only obtained as much esteem from those around you as you have given them, it would not be worthwhile taking all the trouble you do take. You can be very sure that you certainly do not receive more; it is much if you hold in the esteem of others the same place that they hold in yours.

Letter 138. London, 1678

Beware of vanity. Remembrance of the past is a good antidote. Nothing is more to be feared in the spiritual life than what is extraordinary. Everything that inclines you to humility and hatred of self is good.

ON MORTIFICATION

I CAN still sin! Wretched condition of this life! Danger which makes life bitter to all those who love God and who know the value of grace! Yet penance and mortification which can prevent this misery make life sweet! Mortification tames the flesh, weakens inclinations to evil, cuts down occasions of sin, removes enticements, and so on: O holy penance!

Try to make yourself worthy of God's favors by always seeking to refuse nature what it demands both interiorly and exteriorly. Do not be self-willed, but try on the contrary always to do what others wish rather than what you yourself wish, even in indifferent things. Thus you will find that Our Lord is close to you and that your hardness of heart will melt away.

Letter 138. London, 1678

Be on your guard against illusions concerning mortification. Be more obedient on this point than on others.
Sacrifice to God your desire for austerities, and only do
penances which cannot hurt your health: such as interior mortifications.

ON THE DUTIES OF OUR
STATE OF LIFE

Spiritual Reflections

THE good order of things in the world depends upon the fidelity with which each one performs the duties of his state of life. All disorder originates in negligence upon this point. What a grand thing it would be if everyone acquitted himself of his duties! It is, perhaps, the thing that is most neglected even among pious people, indeed probably more often among those than among others. Yet people do not accuse themselves of it. Charles V said to his confessor: "I accuse myself of the sins of Charles, not of those of the Emperor."

More souls are lost for this reason than for any other. Half are damned for not having performed the duties of their state, the other half because others have neglected their duties with regard to them. The duties of one's state take precedence of private duties: for instance, a magistrate must not consider relationship or friendship. Public good must prevail over private good. Jesus Christ, who came into this world to teach us and save us, did not think of his Mother when it was a question of his office as Redeemer: he looked upon others only in so far as they concerned this work of Redemption. Those who cooperated with him are his brothers; those to whom his Precious Blood gives new life are his children; his Mother is she who is perfectly submissive to the will of his Father.

A man who neglects the duties of his state is a discordant voice in the harmony of the world, no matter what else he does. Those who are faithful to all other duties often neglect these; those who do not omit them perform them negligently or through human motives and self-interest. This is not fulfilling their duty.

In choosing a state of life, the human advantages are considered but not the duties. It is impossible to neglect these duties without injuring others, and as God has their interests at heart even more than his own, such neglect is very dangerous.

People would consider it strange for a man to become a religious without knowing to what he was going to bind himself. But what of a secular who has been married for twenty years, or who has held some responsible post in his profession, without knowing the duties these states of life entail.

Sins of omission on this point are easily committed. They are hardly noticed, and consequently reparation is rarely made for them. These are sins that are committed by doing nothing; sins that do not consist in bad actions but which are often the consequence of some good work.

By neglecting your duties, you condemn both yourself and others to punishment: others because you do not teach them their duty and make them fulfill it; and yourself because you do not fulfill your own. The less wicked will be damned for what they have done; the most wicked for what they have omitted to do.

ON THE WORLD

Sermon

WHAT would you say if I asked you if you can live in the world without offending God? When the dangers are put before you of certain kinds of talk, of certain ways of acting, and of backbiting your neighbor, you answer that you cannot help it, that otherwise you would have to be dumb in society, that people talk of nothing else, that you would have to have a heart of bronze to resist all temptations in the midst of a world which breeds them, and that in fact you would have to live like a hermit if you want to escape them.

All this is frequently said in excuse by those who think it justifies them.

It is impossible to frequent the world without offending God, or at any rate without exposing oneself to the danger of offending him: therefore you must renounce the world.

Every Christian has renounced the world and its pomps at baptism. This vow does not oblige you to live like a hermit, but it certainly obliges you to something. It is not an empty promise.

In the world there is an inner world, a second world

96

which every Christian must avoid, for it knows not God and the devil is its ruler. It was of this world that Jesus Christ said: "I pray not for the world" (Jn 17:9). In this world are found those who live solely for vanity and pleasure; it is where the one aim is to please and flatter, where there is hardly anything that is innocent and good, and where people glory in all that ought to make us ashamed.

How foolish to bother about a world full of such unreasonable people. One is proud of a name which he dishonors by a bad life; another prides herself on a dress which she owes to the skill of a dressmaker and which not merely covers a body made of dust but a corrupt soul; another gives up rest and peace to acquire a fortune he does not know how to use; others get furious over things of no importance or things which do not concern them. There is no charity in this world: men are left to die of hunger, while horses and dogs are fed with food that is refused to those who are created in God's image.

The reason why we hear so many complaints about the ingratitude of men is because those to whom we do good are really ungrateful and we ourselves set too high a price on the services we render them.

The trouble we take to please the world is lost. Often when we have had the best intention and made the most effort, the thing fails and no one is grateful for the pains we have taken. We may suffer for years with-

out anyone noticing it; but commit a fault and everyone will be vexed and scold you. To help is not enough;
you must please, and this is not always in our power.
Some have antipathies which make them take offence at
everything certain people do, while a tiny service received
from a favorite is praised and rewarded. This injustice
can be pardoned to those who cannot distinguish natural virtue from real merit, but not to those who like to
serve such a blind master as the world.

ON THE EDUCATION OF CHILDREN

Sermon

DOES it not strike you as a surprising fact that Catholic parents so often urge their children to do what is asked of them from merely human motives and that everything about their homes tends to nourish ambition and luxury? They tell them how such and such a man of obscure birth has made himself famous by his eloquence or has acquired great riches and has married an heiress, that he has built himself a magnificent house and lives envied by all. Such examples are held up to the children, but the parents never think of talking to them of those who are great in the kingdom of heaven. If anyone else tries to speak of these things, the parents stop them as though they would spoil everything by such talk.

There are mothers who take great care of their daughters' health but little of their conscience. Far from forbidding them foolish and even bad books, indecent dresses, undesirable friends, indecent pictures, plays, and dances, they allow them these things and even sometimes force them on their children.

Do not such parents know that spiritual fornication is a crime among Christians; that a look may kill a soul and that a desire or thought is enough to rob children of innocence and grace?

Some mothers think that when they have brought a child into the world they have no further duty toward it. They hand it over to a nurse who may pass on her own bad inclinations to the child with the milk which nourishes it. From the hands of a nurse the child passes into those of a governess or tutor, who has perhaps been chosen without the parents' knowing if the person is good or bad!

Yet marriage was instituted and is blessed only that children may be brought up in the fear of God. If only parents would take the trouble, what could they not do for their children!

*   *   *

If you do not bring up your children well, what *do* you do? It is the only thing you have to do; it is this that God requires of you, for this that he established Christian marriage; and it is on this that you will be judged.

You reply that you have amassed a fortune for your children. Did God ask that of you? At judgment he will say: Give me an account of this soul that I confided to your care. What has become of it? It was the field, the vine that the Lord left in your hands to be cultivated. Have you brought up your children to lead holy lives? What have you taught them? Are they good? Do they fear God? Are they well instructed? Many parents will not know what to answer to these questions. They do not even know if their children are good or bad, well or ill-instructed!

It is surprising how many parents, knowing from their own experience what the world is, and how vain, false, and dangerous the pleasures of this life are, are foolish enough to let their children frequent these pleasures because they themselves are no longer of an age to enjoy them. Such parents, instead of regretting that they have lost their time in such follies and grieving over the sins they have committed, urge their children on toward the same perils. What excuse can they bring forward at judgment to shield themselves from sentence of condemnation? For what grace or mercy can they hope?

ON CHRISTIANS WHO LACK CHRISTIANITY

Sermon

WHEN we look around today on the masses of Christian people, we marvel that such can belong to the chosen race, to those for whom the Word Incarnate suffered and died, to those who know this and know that they are the objects of such care and labor.

God came down from heaven, emptied himself, suffered, and died for each soul. Each Christian soul has been given a re-birth at baptism. God has adopted him for his child. Jesus Christ has cleansed him in his Precious Blood. The Holy Spirit has come upon him in confirmation. To preserve this Christian soul, Jesus Christ has left inexhaustible treasures of merit in his Church: sources of grace in the Sacraments, the sacrifice of the Mass; he has established priests, ceremonies, prayers, blessings: and after all this Christians reduce Christianity to a few exterior practices or even less. Except for these few practices there is no difference between a Christian and a pagan: neither greater decency in dress, nor more frugality in food, nor more reserve in speech, nor more love of God, nor less attachment to the goods and pleasures of this world.

Is it not a thing unworthy of the greatness of God that he who created heaven and earth, angels and men by his word, should have paid so great a price only to have so poor a return from the greater number of Christians?

PART TWO

DIRECTION SUITABLE FOR RELIGIOUS

ON VOCATION

You think it strange that she should embrace a life for which she has no inclination. It seems to me that we never have much inclination for the Cross. I know I had a terrible aversion to religious life when I entered the Society, and I think there are few people who do not experience this repugnance, except those who enter very young, without really knowing what they are doing, and whom God saves from the world because they would not have sufficient strength to overcome the difficulties if they knew about them beforehand.

I am delighted that you love your vocation. I do not know how you judge of this, but the best sign of it is when there is not a single rule or the least regulation that you are not as anxious to observe as exactly as your vows.

ON THE VOWS OF RELIGION

Letter 68. Lyons, 1679

YOUR VOWS are the bonds which are to attach you to
Jesus Christ and his Cross for the rest of your life. They
are sweet bonds, and they must be very dear to you!
Oh, if we could bind ourselves to this loving Spouse by
a million chains instead of by three! Tighten these bonds,
and at the same time break all those, whatever they be,
which attach you to creatures.

Letter 64. Lyons, 1679

Fear nothing in future. Remember you are giving yourself to an all-powerful Spouse; he will be your strength
just as up to now he has been your Peace.

I

ON POVERTY

Letter 1. Lyons, 1674

I recommend you to begin at once to love poverty. How sweet to be able to say to Jesus Christ: My Savior, I possess nothing but thyself, nor even the smallest unnecessary thing. And even among necessary things there is not one to which I am attached. If I felt I was attached to anything but thee, I would deprive myself of it at once and would not tolerate it for a single moment either in my room or on my person.

Letter. Date unknown

Your heavenly Spouse is beautiful above the sons of men, but the beauty is hidden; you will possess him long before you see him; he is of high birth, but the only dowry he asks you to bring is poverty. From him you may expect an ardent and faithful love, but he is as jealous as he is tender.

Retreat Notes. Lyons, 1674

In the meditation upon apostolic poverty I resolved to honor and take pleasure in this virtue all my life, so that

I may always have the consolation of being able to say: I have nothing; whereas the world and self-love find so much satisfaction in possessing and in taking stock of what they possess.

2

ON CHASTITY

Letter 53. Paray, 1676

YOU are vowed to the most loving of all spouses; but remember that he is also the most jealous and that he will not allow your heart to be attached to anything whatsoever.

Be very much on your guard not to allow any earthly love to enter your heart, nor any desire of created things, no matter what they be.

3

ON OBEDIENCE

Letter 105. London, 1678

Our fervor, love of retreat and solitude, of prayer and of austerity must all be ruled by obedience. Make sure that before doing anything extra you do all that God wishes: make yourself dependent from morning till evening, and be quite certain that the most specious [pleasing] and holy things in appearance are horrible in God's eyes as soon as our own will is found in them. A soul which is not submissive in everything like a child is exposed to all the deceits of the devil, who has never deceived and never will deceive a truly obedient soul.

I place so much value upon this virtue that the others seem to me valueless unless they lead to it. I would rather give up all mortifications, prayers, and good works that swerve in a single point, I do not say from the orders, but even from the will of those who govern me, however slight might be the indication of that will. How can we have a single moment of repose if we do our own will? How can we live, even if all we do be holy, if we do not know if what we do be pleasing to God? And how can we know this unless all we do is ordered or approved by Superiors? I say approved and found good: for one can extort permissions and think one is doing marvels when one has forced the Superior to give in to our fervor.

Retreat Notes. Lyons, 1674

The flight into Egypt, from the point of view of mere human prudence, seemed very hard and unreasonable. What was to be done among an unknown and idolatrous people? Yet it is the will of God and therefore must be expedient: to argue about obedience, however unreasonable it seems, is to mistrust the prudence of God and to believe that with all his wisdom he gives orders which cannot be for his glory and our benefit. When orders are given in which humanly we can see no sense, a man of faith rejoices in the thought that it is God who commands and who prepares graces for us which we can only receive in secret ways unknown to us.

Retreat Notes. Lyons, 1674

Sometimes I have felt great repugnance in obeying, but by God's grace I have conquered. I reflected that it is dangerous to make plans for oneself even in things of little importance, unless we are ready to throw them all up in order to obey or to practice charity. There is danger of being humanly attached to any occupation that it costs us to leave off, or that we would rather do than something else, or even rather do than doing nothing. We must consult God about our plans.

Retreat Notes. Lyons, 1674

We may well admire the obedience of Saint Francis Xavier: he is told that he is to make a journey of six thousand miles: he replies that he is ready to start immediately; he did not hesitate a single moment when Saint Ignatius spoke to him—yet he had to leave relations, friends, and country for a foreign land. He did not require to be persuaded. He went without luggage, even without books. He left all joyfully, happy that Saint Ignatius had chosen him. He looked upon it as an opportunity of gaining great merit and believed that God had spoken to him through his Superior.

We, on the contrary, complain if we are asked to do things that are difficult or contrary to our inclinations; we grumble in doing them and think the Superior does not like us. Yet we ought to look upon it as a grace. If we obey only when we like what is commanded, we do it to please ourselves and not for the sake of obedience.

Saint Francis Xavier submitted his judgment. He had little hope of being recalled to Europe, for he was the Apostle of the Indies, the support of religion in half the known world—besides, there seemed no reason to recall him, and he did not expect it.

When we are in a place we like and in which we

think we are doing good, where we are successful in our work and useful to the house, what do we say about an order which calls us elsewhere? But it is just then that we ought to obey: it is God alone who acts against all our human reasoning perhaps, but for reasons which are unknown to us, but which will be very advantageous for us. The worst of it is we will not trust him. But the climate! the Superior! the work! Never mind. Go in God's name: "Cast all your care upon him for he has care of you" (1 Pet 5:7).

ON THE OBSERVANCE
OF THE RULE

Letter 2. Lyons, 1674–1675

I recommend to you an exact and courageous observance of the smallest rules and the least important orders of your Superiors. Nothing is small when it is a question of pleasing God; and it is a great evil to displease him even in very small things. Not long ago I was reading the life of a holy religious (Saint John Berchmans) who, at the hour of death, said he could die with the consolation of never having broken a single rule of his Order or disobeyed a single command of his Superiors however insignificant the things that were ordered. Certainly it requires watchfulness and plenty of resolution to attain to that, but happy the religious who takes it to heart and lives in perfect fidelity. There is nothing impossible with the help of grace, and difficulties do not frighten a courageous heart.

Letter 4. London, 1676

You have a rule; keep it in its completeness; try to omit nothing that it prescribes, and be as strict with yourself about this as if you had made a vow to observe its least details. When it is a question of the rule, be above all human considerations. Give way neither to weakness in pleasing others nor to human respect. This is the only means you have of saving the honor of the profession you have made.

Letter 5. London, 1678

Your rules must take the place of everything until you observe them in every point, so that there is no detail in which you do not comply with what they order. You have no need of a director, nor of direction; consult your rules when you are most fervent, and do not doubt that what God asks of you, by the good inspirations he gives you, can be anything else than inviolable fidelity in doing his will which is marked out for you so exactly in your rules. If people only knew the security and the blessings which are attached to this care in keeping even the least observances, they would make every effort after perfection and their practices of devotion would consist in this alone.

Letter 66. Lyons, 1680

Learn your rule well, and act in such a way that at the hour of your death you may have the consolation of not having broken one deliberately.

Letter 100. London, 1677

It is a great illusion to want to do all one hears of and all one reads in spiritual books and also to keep changing your practices of devotion. Read few books, but study deeply Jesus Christ Crucified. Your rule tells you nearly all you have to do: that is what you ought to cling to. You do not hold the rule from man but from God himself; if you observe it exactly, it is impossible for you not to arrive sooner or later at very great perfection.

Letter 107. London, 1678

Observe your rules perfectly: they are in truth a source of blessings. I confess that mine are my whole treasure and that I find so many blessings enclosed within them that I think, even were I alone on a desert island, I could do without anything else and desire no other help, provided God gave me the grace to observe them perfectly. O holy Rule! Blessed is the soul that loves and cherishes thee and knows what blessings are contained in thee!

Letter 108. London, 1677–1678

How grateful we ought to be to God for giving us a rule to guide us! How blind we are if we think we shall find anything better by withdrawing ourselves from the rule. All our happiness depends upon the respect we have for the least observances. Worldly minds would look upon it as a fetter or a torture. But there is a treasure attached to this exact fidelity, and when it is the outcome of love, a certain sweetness and liberty which is a thousand times more satisfying than the false pleasures of the world.

Retreat Notes. Lyons, 1674

Care in obeying the least observances gives liberty of spirit instead of causing constraint.

Retreat Notes. Lyons, 1674

I have understood this saying of John Berchmans: The greatest mortification is common life. It mortifies both body and mind. Other things are often done through vanity and love of notice. In any case, before doing anything extra I would rather do all ordinary things exactly as the rule prescribes. This goes a long way and leads to great sanctity. In reading the rules, I felt a strong desire to observe them all with God's grace. This demands great fidelity, great courage, great simplicity, great recollection, great strength and constancy, and, above all, a great grace from God.

ON PRAYER

Letter 7. London, 1677

WHAT a mistake it is to be tormented and sad because you have no light or consolation in prayer, to strain your head seeking after sensible devotion at Holy Communion, and to neglect little faults, small observances, and occasions for mortifying your own will and desires, for conquering your human respect and for procuring your own humiliation before others! If we were reasonable, we should think only of these last and not make the slightest effort to succeed according to our own ideas; because, as a matter of fact, we never succeed better than when we humbly endure dryness and the privation of this false fervor that nature so loves and that the real love of God despises and even rejects as far as it is able.

Letter 74. London, 1677

If you were ravished in ecstasy twenty-four times a day and I had twenty-four distractions in saying a Hail Mary, but if I were as humble and mortified as you, I would not change my involuntary distractions for all your ecstasies which have no merit. In a word: there is no devotion without mortification. You must always do violence to yourself, especially interiorly. Never allow nature to be mistress, nor your heart to be attached to anything, no matter what it may be; and then I would canonize you and not even ask you how you prayed.

Letter 71. London, 1678

If you only pray when you are obliged or because you are obliged, you will never succeed in prayer, nor will you ever love it, nor ever take pleasure in intimate converse with God.

A soul which exempts herself from prayer when ill or upset through fear of harming herself, does not know how to pray; for, far from harming, it strengthens both mind and heart, it keeps the soul in peace and leaves behind it a consolation which relieves all trouble.

It is neither vows nor promises which should attract you to this holy exercise but the happiness that a faithful soul finds in approaching to her God. I pray that the Holy Spirit may give you the gift of prayer: it is the hidden treasure of the Gospel; but to possess it we must detach ourselves from everything that we may enjoy God and merit his caresses.

ON PEACE OF SOUL

Letter 2. Lyons, 1674–1675

FROM the moment one has a real desire of giving oneself entirely to God, one enjoys great peace. I am sure that which you have found by Our Lord's mercy is the result of the sincere and fervent will which he has given you to serve him and belong to him without reserve. You would indeed be miserable if there were anything in the world that could trouble you, for there is nothing that can prevent you from becoming a saint, in fact everything may help you to become one. There is nothing, not even our sins, from which we may not gain advantage for our sanctification, through the knowledge they give us of ourselves and by the renewal of fervor with which they inspire us. This being so, I do not see what could happen that could prevent you gaining profit if only you have enough faith to realize that nothing happens to you except by God's permission and enough submission to conform yourself to his will. If ever you have a fit of sadness or trouble, remember that it is because you are still attached to life, or health, or some comfort, or person, or thing that you ought to forget and despise that you may desire Jesus

Christ only. Every time your heart feels troubled, be sure that it is caused by some unmortified passion and that it is a fruit of self-love which is not yet dead. Thinking this, throw yourself at the feet of Jesus Crucified, and say: My Savior, do I still desire something which is not thee? Art thou not sufficient for me, shall I not love thee alone and be content to be loved only by thee? What have I come to seek, O my God, if not thee? Can I not keep thee? What does it matter what they say of me, or if I am loved or despised, well or ill, occupied with this work or with that, placed with these people or with others? Provided that I am with thee, and thou with me, I am content.

Letter 53. Paray, 1676

Remember that the facility you find today in doing your duty may soon be changed into great interior trials. Be ready for everything. Have a firm confidence that in whatever state God is pleased to place you, he will never fail to grant you great help. You are his. Henceforth he looks upon you as his property which it is to his interests to care for, so, provided that you do not give yourself to another, he will never allow anything to happen that can harm you, or anything that you cannot turn to your advantage if you will to do so.

Letter 91. Lyons, 1679–1680

Cherish great confidence in God and a sincere desire to do his will. I am sure your obedience will save you. Cling closely and constantly to this obedience, and laugh at the vain fears your enemy suggests concerning the future. He is strangely afraid of the sacrifice you are about to make, and as, until it is made, he will not despair of preventing you from attaining the goal to which Our Lord is leading you, he will not cease tormenting you until you are bound by indissoluble bonds to Jesus Christ and to his Cross.

Letter 61. Lyons, 1679

Learn this lesson well, once for all: God is the only Master of our hearts; he alone can give solid peace, and our whole confidence must rest in him only.

ON FERVOR

Letter 7. London, 1677

YOU say that if you could see me more often you would be better than you are. Perhaps you have not sufficiently considered that in your convent you have him from whom all grace comes, without whose help no one can help you, and who has no need of me or of anyone else to sanctify you. Think about this and say no more about it, because there is nothing to be said. It is only our want of confidence that prevents us from profiting by the presence of Jesus Christ, who does not remain with us in order to do nothing! We so seldom have recourse to him and we have so little faith that it is no wonder if we share so little in the treasures of light and grace which he communicates to those who have recourse to him as the Master and Source of all perfection.

Secondly, I fear you are looking upon lack of sensible and interior consolation as a want of fervor, so that finding yourself dry, you lose courage and fall into faults for which you do not immediately make reparation, and this leads to tepidity. Then you imagine that in order to begin again holily, as one does when full of fervor and devotion, it is necessary for you to feel the fervor you have lost. But the contrary is the case: in order to bring back fervor you must begin by humbling yourself and by practicing mortification just as though you were urged on by sensible consolation. It is not fervor which makes people humble, charitable, regular, and mortified, but the practice of these virtues which makes them fervent.

ON GENEROSITY IN GOD'S SERVICE

Retreat Notes. Lyons, 1674

MANY reasons convince me that I must aim at it (generosity) with all my strength. First, God has loved me too well for me to spare myself henceforth in his service: the mere thought of doing so horrifies me. What! not belong to God wholly after his mercy toward me, or reserve something for myself after all that I have received from him? Never will my heart consent to act thus.

Secondly, when I see of how little account I am, and what it is I can do for God's glory by employing myself entirely in his service, I am ashamed at the mere thought of depriving him of anything.

Thirdly, there would be no safety for me in any half-measures: I know myself, and I should soon fall into a bad extreme.

Fourthly, only those who have given themselves to God unreservedly can expect to die calmly.

Fifthly, they alone lead a peaceful and tranquil life.

Sixthly, in order to do much for God, one must be completely his. However little you keep back, you will be unfit to do great things for others.

Seventhly, in this state one maintains a lively faith and a firm hope, one asks God confidently and one obtains infallibly.

ON PUSILLANIMITY

Letter 74. London, 1677

I think you are somewhat slow and pusillanimous.
If you are, you will recognize it by these marks: if
you are tempted to postpone what you are obliged
to do or what you have resolved to do; if you leave
off something good that you have begun; if you often
change your methods and practices of devotion; if you
imagine that things are beyond you and only fit for
great saints; if you omit to do something from human
respect, through fear of appearing better than you
are, fear of importuning Superiors, fear lest it should
seem you were condemning others, fear of mortifying
others; if you are not absolutely sincere with those
to whom you ought to disclose your conscience; if
you persuade yourelf to be content with a mediocre
fervor; if you allow yourself to think that anything
in obedience is small, that a word does not count,
that you can put off obeying instantly, take another
stitch, and so on.

The remedy is not to pardon oneself anything;
not to listen to any repugnance; to try always to

conquer self and to be quite convinced that one great reason for doing a thing is because you find difficulty in it, and for not doing it because you are inclined to do it, always supposing that you do nothing against obedience.

ON TEPIDITY

Letter 4. London, 1676

YOU ask me to write to you on the subject of tepidity and hardness of heart. Do you want a sermon, or do you expect me to send you a book instead of a letter? If it were true, which I cannot believe, that you are in the state you write of, you would require far more powerful instruments than those to draw you out of it and I should have no hope that either my prayers or my exhortations would avail.

I would rather have a great sinner to convert than a religious who has fallen into tepidity. It is an evil almost without remedy. Few surmount it; age which cures other faults only augments this. I have sometimes found in the same convent nuns who, through lack of vocation, have lived most worldly lives in religion, and others who, while doing nothing to scandalize anyone, have been totally lacking in fervor and zeal for their perfection. In three months I had the consolation of seeing the former live in most perfect regularity, constantly aiming at mortification and union with God, while many months and even years have not sufficed to rouse the latter from their sloth and make them practice things which were trifles compared to what the others did.

This evil of tepidity is only too common. Religious houses are full of people who keep the rule: rise, go to Mass, meditation, confession and Communion, because it is the custom, because the bell rings and the others go; they do all this and more without any interior devotion, without either attention or desire to please God; if they purify their intention, it is done rather from routine than from any real fervor of spirit. They put no heart into what they do; they have their own little ideas and plans which occupy them; they are indifferent to the things of God. Their relations and their friends both inside and outside the convent absorb all their affections, so that nothing is left for God but a few forced and grudging acts which cannot be acceptable to him. Such people have consciences which are in no way disturbed by a hundred things which would trouble souls that fear God. They murmur and foster feelings of aversion and revolt against Superiors; they overlook faults against poverty; they deliberately resolve not to bother about little things nor about advancing in perfection; thus living, they go to confession and to Holy Communion without any desire of amendment; sins are confessed as though they were merely a tale of little interest; the sacred tribunal of penance is approached, not with the sentiments of contrition and humility that one ought to have, but merely because it is the day for confession and one's turn to go, and on leaving the confessional silence is broken and murmuring begins again, so that after one, two, or three years, it is seen that the negligent are still negligent, the slack still slack, the bad-tempered have not become gentle, nor the proud humble, the lazy are still lacking in fervor and the selfish in detachment, and so of the rest. Such communities, which ought to be furnaces where all can enkindle their love of God and purify their souls more and more, remain always in this terrible lukewarmness, if indeed they do not go from bad to worse! If you want to live like that, it is better to remain in the world where perhaps you will run less risk of losing your soul!

ON CHRIST OUR FRIEND ABOVE ALL

Spiritual Reflections

JESUS, thou art my only true and real friend. Thou dost share all my sorrows and takest them upon thyself, knowing how to turn them to my good. Thou dost listen to me kindly when I tell thee of my difficulties, and thou never failest to lighten them. Wherever I go I always find thee; thou dost never leave me, and if I am obliged to go away, I find thee waiting for me.

Thou art never weary of listening to me, and thou dost never cease to do me good. I am sure of being loved if I love thee. Thou hast no need of me or of my goods, and thou dost not deprive thyself by giving me of thy riches. However wretched I am, no one nobler or more clever or even more holy can rob me of thy friendship; and death which separates us from all other friends will only unite me to thee. All the accidents of age or of fortune will never detach thee from me; on the contrary, I shall never enjoy thee more fully and thou wilt never be so close to me as when everything goes against me. Thou dost bear with my defects with tender patience; even my infidelities and ingratitude do not wound thee in such a way that thou art not always ready to return to me when I call upon thee.

Retreat Notes. Lyons, 1674

Jesus is in the midst of us in the Blessed Sacrament. What a consolation to live in the same house where he dwells! Yet does it not often seem as though we ignored this happiness? Do we often visit him? Do we go to him in our needs and consult him in our plans? Do we bring him our little sorrows instead of talking about them and complaining and murmuring to others? "There hath stood one in the midst of you whom you know not" (Jn 1:26).

Spiritual Notes. Lyons, 1674

You love the King although you have never seen him and probably never will see him, although he has no affection for you and does not even know you, and if he did know you he would take no notice of you. Yet we find it hard to love God, whom we do not see, it is true, but whom we shall see throughout eternity and who sees us, and loves us, and does us good, and who knows our most secret thoughts! You say you love the King because he is your Master. But God is much more than this: he is our Creator, our Father.

Spiritual Notes. Lyons, 1674

I feel myself moved to imitate the simplicity of God in my affections, loving him only, cherishing no other love but this, which is easy since I find in God all that I can love elsewhere.

But my friends: they love me and I love them. Thou seest this and I feel it, O my God, who art alone good, alone lovable. Must I sacrifice these to thee since thou desirest to have me entirely? I will make this sacrifice with my whole heart, since thou dost forbid me to share my friendship with any creature. Accept this painful sacrifice, but in exchange, my divine Savior, be thou their friend. As thou wilt take their place with me, take my place with them. I will remind thee of them daily in my prayers, and of what thou owest them in me in promising to be my substitute. Jesus, be thou their friend, their sole and real friend! Jesus, be my friend, since thou commandest me to be thine.

Letter 66. Lyons, 1680

As Jesus Christ possesses your whole heart, he wishes also to have all your anxieties and all your thoughts. Think of him and trust in his goodness for all the rest. You will see that he will make all things right when you think only of his interests. Reflect very specially on this advice: it contains a great treasure. Experience will show you that I am not deceiving you.

Letter 74. London, 1678

Do not let your peace depend upon what is outside you; you will see that Our Lord will supply for everything when you are satisfied with him alone, and you will find more in him than in all creatures together. Beware of thinking that you have need of anyone whom God withdraws from you. He is too faithful to take away from you any help that he sees necessary for you, so that you may reach the perfection he expects from you.

Retreat Notes. Lyons, 1674

My Savior, do I still desire something which is not thee? Art thou not sufficient for me, shall I not love thee alone and be content to be loved only by thee! What have I come here to seek, O my God, if it be not thee? What does it matter what they say of me, or if I am loved or despised, well or ill, occupied with this work or with that, placed with these people or with those? Provided that I am with thee, and thou with me, I am content.

ON MAKING A RETREAT

Letter 79. Paray, 1681

CHOOSE a suitable book and subjects of meditation. To draw fruit from the retreat it should be as complete as possible: that is to say, no conversation, however holy, should interrupt it, except with the director or the Superior if she wishes it and it is necessary. Make a time-table for the employment of your time, and be very exact in keeping to it. Read little. Do not expect interior consolation, but be ready for aridity, weariness, and other crosses that God may please to send you. Be firmly resolved to listen to God and to follow him as far as he may lead you. Great lights are not always received in time of prayer, but often at other times if you are faithful in using your time as prescribed.

It is important to undertake this retreat more seriously than you have perhaps hitherto done, so as to examine in good faith if prudence and piety demand anything more from you either now or for the future, anything that perhaps you may have neglected up to now through want of thought. What is it a question of? Is it of any consequence? Can I be too careful about it? Upon what is my confidence founded? Why do I delay?

Am I not risking too much through lack of precaution? What am I risking? Use your reason about the one thing in the world you should have at heart, the one thing for which our reason has been given to us. You must live as a saint—I do not say till death, but at least for eight days. The least infidelity might spoil everything and put an obstacle to the graces God has prepared for you.

Yet you must take care of your health; the greatest mortifications are those of the mind and heart; do not allow these any satisfaction during your retreat if you want God to allow you to feel the unction of his grace.

Instruction given to the Students of the Jesuit College, Lyons, in 1680

1. The Spiritual Exercises should be made only at certain times when the soul, drawn by God to solitude through contempt of the things of this world, or by some special attraction of grace which urges it to holiness and reformation of life, seeks the means of satisfying this desire, or else when grieved at the sinfulness of its life it is touched by a desire of real penance.

2. At these times a retreat should be made so that we may have time to examine our interior life and see what God exacts of us and how we may carry it out.

3. It is a very good thing to make a retreat in order to change our life and become holy, but for those who

have not these dispositions, I think it is a good thing to make the Exercises so that they may examine the state of their soul and see if they are in the way of salvation; if, living as they do, they run no risks for eternity; if there is anything to change or if they can continue peacefully in the way in which they are walking.

4. Those in retreat should give themselves up to it completely and admit no other business whatsoever. It is but just that we should give to God and to our soul all the application that is called for by the most important affairs of life.

5. Entire solitude is necessary.

6. There must be great purity of heart and a perfect keeping of all Rules and Additions: it is only for eight days. A small fault may place a great obstacle to the lights God gives us and cause him to withdraw.

7. A great indifference as to consolation is also necessary. We must not expect it but make up our mind to suffer every sort of weariness, dryness and desolation. We deserve these things; if it pleases God to send them to us we shall have eight days of patience and penance.

8. If we cannot make up our mind to become holy during retreat, we must at least resolve to correspond to the graces it may please God to give us and not resist the good inspirations that the Holy Spirit may give us.

My God I have no desire for great holiness, perhaps I have even a dread of it; but if in thy mercy thou wilt change me, give me courage and detach me thyself from the world, at least let me put no obstacle in thy way. Thou knowest what means to take so as to win my heart; these means are in thy hands, thou art the Master. Holiness frightens me; thou canst cure me of this false and foolish fear and make all easy to me that seems so difficult. Thou alone canst do this.

9. Great confidence in God. He sought me in the midst of the world and its occupations when I fled from him; he will not abandon me now that I seek him in retreat, or now when at least I do not flee from him.

10. We must also have great humility in making known our conscience to the director of the retreat, even if we have nothing else to say but that we feel nothing, see nothing, and are not drawn toward anything good; we need humility also in keeping to the meditations and reading prescribed even when we think something else would suit us better. This simplicity is very meritorious and draws down great blessings.

11. On the eve of the retreat we must arouse a desire of solitude in our heart: "Who will give me wings?" (see Ps 55:6–7) and the desire also of holiness: "Blessed are they that hunger and thirst after justice for they shall have their fill" (Mt 5:6).

ON A CHANGE OF SUPERIOR

Letter 75. London, 1678

No doubt you will lose much in losing your present Superior. But if your confidence rested in her, it is good for you that she should go; if it rests on God, he has plenty of means of helping you, after taking her help away. Offer the sorrow of this separation in reparation for the time in which you have not made good use of her maternal guidance; and have confidence that by this resignation you will expiate all the faults you have committed in her regard.

It does not matter what sort of character the new Superior has. God blesses simplicity and obedience, whatever the Superior may be like.

LETTER OF SAINT CLAUDE DE LA COLOMBIÈRE TO HIS SISTER MARGUERITE-ELIZABETH DE LA COLOMBIÈRE, RELIGIOUS OF THE VISITATION CONVENT AT CONDRIEU, LYONS, 1674

MY VERY DEAR SISTER,

I have just heard news about you that has delighted me, because I am told that you are perfectly happy. May God be praised! You would have to be miserable indeed not to find happiness with such a good Master as he to whom you have given yourself. Your happiness will grow in the measure in which you detach your heart from all earthly things so as to consecrate it entirely to God. I have only one fear, and that is that your love of a quiet life and the natural horror you have of noise and fuss are partly the cause of the joy you are experiencing. If this is so, your joy is a false joy; in the state of life you have embraced it is the cross you must seek and love, the cross that crucifies: that is to say, the cross that is most contrary to your natural inclinations. It is difficult to avoid crosses of this sort: in community life there is always something that goes against the grain and rubs up against our humors and fancies. We must be on our guard to profit by these precious occasions and to submit our will and judgment in everything. Unless we do this, we shall never enjoy perfect peace, or at least not for any length of time.

I think you are extremely fortunate in having entered a house where virtue and such perfect charity reign; but if it were not so, I know that it need not hinder a fervent soul that seeks God alone. Besides the fact that we think little of the faults of others when we are occupied in correcting our own, everything helps those who are of good will, and the bad examples which corrupt the weak only urge on those who love Our Lord by the desire they inspire to make reparation to him for all he suffers from the negligent and from the fear we have of becoming like them. Nevertheless, it is an advantage to be surrounded by holy examples and to have before our eyes models of virtue who animate us to good and reproach us for our shortcomings; some such are always to be found in large communities. In any case, if the living fail, we may always learn from the dead. This is why I think it would be a good thing for you to read the lives of the holy members of your Order or even those of religious who have followed a different rule and who have attained to sanctity. I am supposing that your Superiors approve of this, for it would be better to remain idle, so to speak, than to do anything without their approval. Supposing, however, they consent, apply yourself to this reading, and note the paths in which the saints have walked, so that by God's grace you too may arrive at the perfection they acquired. You will find that they did very few things that you cannot do, helped by the same grace.

I have only one other thing to say to you, but it is essential and I pray with all my heart that it may never leave your mind and heart, because I know you will be happy all your life if you practice it. Remember that you only entered religion to save your own soul—yours in particular—and to prepare yourself to give an account to God, when it shall please him to call you to himself. This must be your sole care. You will be judged on your rule and on your vows. Be always ready to give an account of the way you have kept them. Let your sisters live as they please; that is not your business. What a horrible temptation it is to meddle with what concerns others! Let Superiors govern as they think fit. Why should you bother about it? Let it be enough for you to know what is asked of yourself, and whether it appears reasonable to you or not, as long as there is no evident sin, it is God himself who commands you. Such and such a thing that you consider worthy of blame is perhaps that which God deems most necessary for your sanctification. A Superior may govern badly; but it is impossible for God not to govern you well through her. O dearest Sister, fix this well in your mind. If you do not seize this principle well, you will lose your time in religion because your whole life there is one of obedience. Now this obedience has no merit when it is not rendered to God in the person whom he has put in his place; it is quite certain that it is not God we have in view if we judge, examine, and, above all, condemn that which has been ordered. When the Holy Spirit reigns within us, he inspires us with a childlike simplicity which finds everything good and reasonable, or, if you like it better, with a divine prudence which shows us God in everything, which recognizes and acknowledges him in all who represent him, even in those who are the least virtuous and who have the fewest natural and supernatural gifts.

I write all this to you because, as you have entered later than many others, you may be tempted in this way. But the more sense you have, the more submissive you should be in spirit, for there is nothing more reasonable than to allow oneself to be governed by God in whatever way he sees good and by whomever he pleases. It should not be more difficult for a good religious to obey a child than the Founder of the Order if he were still living, or even Our Lady herself if she were visibly to undertake the direction of the house.

Here is a whole sermon, but do not look upon it as most pious discourses are looked upon, merely as beautiful thoughts spoken at random. I write what I feel because of my affection for you and because I long so much for you to be a saint. I should be wretched if you did not think seriously of becoming one, and I do not think I could make up my mind ever to see you or to write to you if I knew you would be content with mediocrity.

LA COLOMBIÈRE.